Emerging Proud Press
The Enterprise Centre
Norwich  NR4 7TJ
United Kingdom

ISBN: 978-1-9160860-4-3 (Print)
ISBN: 978-1-9160860-5-0 (Ebook)
www.EmergingProud.com

D1393114

Stories of Hope & Transformation

# DEDICATION

This book is dedicated to all brave souls around the world who have been affected by the painful consequences of suicide. May your light continue to shine even on your darkest days, and let us never forget those for whom the world became too painful and are sadly no longer with us.

"Place your hand over your heart, can you feel it? That is called purpose. You're alive for a reason; don't ever give up. The world is a better place for you being in it."

— Unknown

All stories contained in this Pocket Book are works of memoir, however, some elements may have been fictionalised. Some names may have been changed to avoid identification. We cannot be held liable for any falsehoods, published by us in good faith, as given to us by the story contributors, including any claims to qualifications, etc. made by story contributors in their personal bios.

We have chosen to keep the stories in the style of each contributor's original submission as much as possible, and native spellings have been used for editing purposes, e.g. we have used both UK and US English throughout the book, according to where the Experiencer lives.

The demographics of the story-tellers are a natural consequence of who came forward to tell their story, and have not been intended as a particular representation of gender, ethnicity, sexuality or religion. We aim to be an inclusive, non-discriminatory project, and we do not align with any one religious or other belief over another.

Any healing modalities, story contributors' personal publications and services, or other resources mentioned within this book are not necessarily endorsed by the KindaProud team or project. If you are intending to make any significant lifestyle or medication changes as a result of being inspired by reading anyone's story, please seek professional medical advice before doing so.

This project is dedicated to maintaining the integrity of the voices of the people that have shared their stories.

The stories shared are real life situations and some of them may contain language that could be triggering for some people, such as suicidal behaviour, violence and upsetting content. We recognise that each individual taking part in the project and reading this book will be at different stages of their transformation journey, and we want to honour that where we're all at is perfectly okay. If you are at all triggered by reading the stories, please seek support from the 'Resources' section in the back of the book.

# Praise for this KindaProud Pocket Book

**"Courage is what it takes to stand up and speak
Courage is what it takes to sit down and listen"**

## — Winston Churchill

*After reading this book, this statement speaks to me, and I'm sure for anyone else who reads the incredible life stories; the hardships, struggles, the strength of the human spirit and the ability to be faced with the worst possible situations a person could be faced with, and the incredible outcome of each person's experience.*

*As a Samaritan, we listen and support people who are experiencing suicidal thoughts and feelings, being non judgemental, respecting self-determination. We are a safe place to talk honestly and openly 24 hours and 7 days a week. Our contact details are in the back of the book.*

*I feel this book is a testament to the determination of the people I have read about, it has truly touched my heart and I'm sure you'll feel the same way that I do when you read it.*

T. Northwest Samaritans UK

*People contemplate suicide when they believe they have no hope left. These moving and powerful stories show that despair can be the beginning, not the end, and can open up the path to a new, meaningful and rewarding life. The evidence is in the words of these 16 courageous individuals. They have lessons for all of us, but particularly for those struggling with hopelessness and despair.*

Dr Lucy Johnstone, Consultant Clinical Psychologist, author and the former Programme Director of the Bristol Clinical Psychology Doctorate and was the lead author of *Good practice guidelines on the use of psychological formulation (Division of Clinical Psychology, 2011)*. She has worked in Adult Mental Health settings for many years, most recently in a service in South Wales. She was lead author, along with Professor Mary Boyle, for the *Power Threat Meaning Framework*, a Division of Clinical Psychology-funded project to outline a conceptual alternative to psychiatric diagnosis, which was published in January 2018.

*Sometimes, if we look hard enough amongst the barrage of biomedical model messages about 'mental health' and human suffering that this society is swamped with, we find books like this.*

*Books that give a voice to individuals, that celebrates the strength of the human spirit and our connection with each other.*

*These courageous testimonies remind us, unequivocally, that the route to 'healing' (or whatever word we choose to use), is in finding our own meaning, making our own sense and telling our own stories.*

Jo Watson, Psychotherapist and Activist.

Founder of Drop the Disorder FaceBook group and Organiser of the 'A Disorder for Everyone!' events. www.adisorder4everyone.com

*The incredible stories captured in the pages of this KindaProud Pocketbook of Hope remind us all what human beings have always known, but what over time has been forgotten; mental and emotional distress provides the crucible of transformation, always on our side and never against us. It is only by reaching their perceived rock bottom, that these 16 incredible souls are able to finally find their ground and a pathway leading them, not to the life that they had planned, but rather to the life they were always meant to be living.*

Joanna, Phyllida & James, Co-Founders, Safely Held Spaces https://www.safelyheldspaces.org

# Brought Back from the Brink

If I could see what life might bring
If I could only see the way
If things lined up to mean something
Would that push the sad away?

Would that help me see what I
Would do with my time left here
Would the life that may be nigh
Bring joy for me much nearer

As each day for me unfolds
As my mind begins to clear
As my story yet untold
Becomes the only thing I hear

I realise life waits for me
I need to grasp it with both hands
I cannot let myself un-be
Whilst my real life before me stands

— Ambriel

# Contents

# About KindaProud

## Our KindaProud Pocket Book series Ethos and Message

Why do we need 'KindaProud' Pocket Books of Hope and Transformation? There is a rising epidemic of mental health problems in our society, and alongside it a pervasive negative prognosis message that goes out to those who are struggling emotionally. It's our shared belief, due to our personal experiences, that one of the most important elements of getting back on a road to recovery (and ultimately transformation) is to hear personal stories of HOPE from those who have been there before and not just survived, but thrived.

Each Pocket Book has its own KindaProud Rep; a Peer who has personal experience of 'coming through' the theme of that specific book. These are the first 4 books currently in the series:-

- #Emerging Proud through NOTEs (Non-Ordinary Transcendent Experiences)

- #Emerging Proud through Disordered Eating, Poor Body Image and Low Self- Esteem

- #Emerging Proud through Suicide

- #Emerging Proud through Trauma and Abuse

## What are the main Aims and Objectives of the KindaProud Pocket Book series?

To relieve people of the distress associated with transformational crises by offering authentic examples of personal stories and resources to engender hope and initiate recovery.

To decrease stigma, improve wellbeing and influence the saving of lives by providing a more compassionate and positive conceptual framework for emotional distress.

To use the profits from book sales to continue to distribute free books, and hence messages of HOPE, to mental health facilities, and those in need, all around the world.

All of the stories in this book have been kindly donated by peers who have personally experienced this specific theme of distress and 'emerged transformed'; dedicated to giving hope that there is light at the end of the tunnel to others who may still be suffering. This book series is totally not-for-profit, was seed-funded by *The Missing Kind charity*, and continues to be supported voluntarily through the endless dedication of each peer Rep, our Ambassador and Publisher Sean Patrick of *That Guy's House* who supported us to set up #Emerging Proud Press, and Jenna Gould, our 'PR Guru' of *Media Jems*.

# Meet Sean our Publisher and Ambassador!

I guess you could say that I was a typical Millennial/Gen Y kind of guy. I lived life on the 'ordinary' path; going from High School to College to University to my first job in the City. Embracing all of the joys of young professional city life (like I'd seen so much on TV growing up), however, having the curse of also knowing that my life needed to have meaning and without it I was doomed. And so, right on time, feelings of anxiety and depression became present in my early 20s, with social anxiety leading on to more serious depression.

Like many people I didn't know where I fitted into the

world, and despite having the things I was 'supposed to', I felt unhappy, anxious and unfulfilled. I felt like I was on a treadmill and scared by the world.

My 'crisis point' hit when I started to experience severe panic attacks at 22 years old. It was then that I had no option but to admit I had problems that at that time I couldn't rationalise with my own intellect or understanding. In other words, I was having a mental health crisis.

I started by reading books, gaining a better understanding of my own mind, and ultimately found a more spiritual outlook on life through daily meditation and adopting spiritual beliefs. I had read these books from the age of 15 so it was 'old hat' for me. However, a 22-year-old having a crisis could engage with them with much more desperation than a 15-year-old wanting to be *his best self.*

After accepting an expat job in Hong Kong and spending half a year away from my 'ordinary life', I had the chance to recalibrate, explore meditation and mindfulness, and let go of damaging old patterns and beliefs.

I turned my life upside down.

On returning home, I set up a blog called *That Guy Who Loves The Universe* and began to share ideas about spirituality and positive mental health with my following, which grew to over 15,000 people. I began to speak at conferences and wellness events all over the world and released an Amazon bestseller in July 2016. My mess latterly became my message.

In 2017, I developed my own wellness company, *That Guy's House,* with a main focus on wellness books and mental health projects.

After meeting Katie, the project's Founder, via a synchronistic introduction by our *#Emerging Proud through Suicide* book Rep., Kelly, and finding out more about the #Emerging Proud campaign, Katie and I both knew that bringing our personal experiences and skills together to launch the KindaProud series of Pocket Books would be the perfect collaboration

# Meet the Project's Founder

My name is Katie Mottram and I'm the Founder of the #Emerging Proud campaign, through which the KindaProud book series has been birthed. #Emerging Proud is a grassroots social movement aimed at: 'Re-framing mental distress as a catalyst for positive transformation'; providing a platform for people who have 'emerged transformed' through a personal crisis and feel called to share their story and give hope to others.

I was called to start this movement due to finding that re-framing my own crisis as a transformational growth process (which still continues!), and hearing the experiences of others, was the thing that helped me to connect with my authentic Self, and start to live the life I was born to live.

When I experienced a personal crisis in 2008, what I needed was a message of HOPE, that all would be okay, not that there was anything 'wrong' with me. I needed to connect with others who had been through similar challenges and were able to walk alongside me whilst I found my own way out of the darkness.

In the last decade, it has been through my own research; looking at more empowering ways of understanding what happened to me, my reactions to it, and how to go about self-healing, in addition to connecting with my amazing peers and listening to their stories, that has really set me on my own path of transformation. This feels like the complete opposite of what I had been told was helpful whilst working within mental health services for 15 years previously. Hence my passion to provide others with the tools that helped me not only to survive, but to thrive and love life.

You can read my full story in my own book, *Mend the Gap: A transformative journey from deep despair to spiritual awakening*, which I published in 2014.

I truly hope that this book, and the others in the 'Pocket Books of Hope and Transformation' series, inspires and supports you in your own evolutionary journey...

And, remember: let that light you hold deep inside shine unapologetically bright - we were ALL born to shine our light in the world - in whatever way that feels right to you!

Find out more about the campaign and what we're up to at: **www.emergingproud.com**

# Meet our Peer Pocket Book Rep,
# Kelly Walsh

*Kelly Walsh exudes positivity; if you met her now it would be hard to believe that she's experienced not only the survival of her own suicide attempt, but also been bereaved by the suicide of her father. Kelly now perceives these experiences as making her the person she is today: proud and full of unconditional love.*

*We are so honoured to have Kelly as our KindaProud Rep for the Pocket Book of Hope and Transformation: #Emerging Proud through Suicide. Kelly is a true inspiration and through not professing to be perfectly 'healed' but on her healing journey, she is a perfect example of the transformative power of crises...*

## Ending the Taboo of Suicide

Suicide, a subject often misunderstood, rarely openly talked about and, in many cases, the cause of much pain, shame, guilt, blame and ultimately deep-rooted fear. Fear of what others may think; fear of a dark, guilty secret getting out; fear of the world knowing you or someone close to you tried to, or actually did, end their physical life through suicide.

But, and this is a BIG but, it doesn't have to be this way. Suicide in my case was not the end and, for various reasons, was just the beginning. The beginning of an incredible healing journey that continues to this day; and the acknowledgement and understanding that unconditional love holds no bounds.

I write from my heart and soul, as a survivor of my own suicide attempt and as a loving daughter whose dear father transitioned home to spirit via hanging 6 years later.

Today I stand tall and proud that I not only survived suicide but also thrived. Thrived in the midst of adversity, thrived in the midst of deep pain and anguish, and thrived during the days and nights when the world seemed so dark, un-loving and lonely.

## My suicide attempt

Like a lot of people I have suppressed trauma to heal. In 2009 I took a huge overdose and tried to end my physical life. In hospital I had a profound spiritual experience, travelled through 7 dimensions, experienced the 'oneness' of the universe and the unconditional healing power of Divine Love, and was told by Divinity that it wasn't my time. The message I was given during this NDE (near-death experience) is that 'love will heal and transform the world'. I came round from my experience with my arms across my chest and opened them in slow motion and proclaimed that I had met God and angels. The following evening I received a vision and shouted out 9 poignant words:

**'Like-minded souls will collaborate to change the world!'**

These powerful words have never left me and deep in my heart and soul I knew one day I would be sharing my experience, in collaboration with others, to the wider world. I now feel I am acting on my soul's purpose but it hasn't always been that way. Like a lot of people who have had profound spiritual experiences I didn't initially feel mentally strong enough to talk openly about what had happened to me through fear of rejection or potential ridicule. I tried desperately to forget what had happened and focus on rebuilding my life.

A number of years later I realised that trying to

suppress what had happened to me was no longer an option. It had happened, it was part of my soul's journey and I had to deal with the emotional rollercoaster connected to my experience in the best way I could. My life was never going to be the same again. My primary focus was to try and integrate my experience into my daily life, whilst exploring ways of sharing the love, wisdom and knowledge I gained during my brief visit to the 'other side'. Little did I know that my experience, and the understanding it gave me, would prepare me for one of the most painful experiences I was going to endure in my earthly life: the transition of my father, David Walsh, by suicide in September 2015.

The pain I felt when we received the telephone call to say he had hung himself is indescribable. However, I truly believe that what I learned during my experience, and the subsequent spiritual and healing path I have been on since, has helped me to cope with this tragedy in a far more peaceful manner than I could have done otherwise. I also gain further strength in 'the knowing' that my dad is still very much around me and that one day we will be reunited again.

Losing dad has not been an easy process but in many ways it has helped me grow in character. I now recognise that since childhood I have been seeking love and acceptance outside of myself when the only person I really needed to seek that from was me. My life experiences to date, including the pain and suffering, have made me who I am and I wouldn't change a thing. I believe I chose this path coming into this world so that one day I would be in a position to help others with their healing journey to self-love and self-acceptance. I am particularly passionate about raising awareness of suicide and speaking openly and honestly about my experience at both ends of the spectrum.

I really feel more suicides could be prevented if people understood that it is impossible to end their life, as our soul and spirit continues with the same issues we were having difficulty with here on the earth plane, and at some point they will still need to be dealt with, either in the various dimensions or during their next incarnation.

This knowing, gained from my near-death experience, has saved my life on numerous occasions. Periodically, my trauma resurfaces and it often manifests in severe episodes of anxiety. The pain can be so intense: it feels like a metal vice is clamping down on my forehead and I can only describe it as a form of torture. My most recent bout of anxiety had me in tears daily for 6 weeks; I just wanted the mental pain and anguish to go away. Thoughts of suicide played on my mind, but fortunately my personal knowledge and understanding has always kept me earth-bound, even at my lowest ebbs.

I know that, no matter what, it is better to stay in the physical realm with my loved ones around me and work through my pain and perceived problems so that I can continue to work on what needs to be healed rather than end my physical life. Like most people, I have never really wanted to die and in truth have only wanted the pain to stop.

I share my personal experiences and the message of divinity's unconditional love to help individuals who may be suffering. My dream is to offer hope to anyone who may be suicidal and also to those who have lost their loved ones to suicide, by affirming that they are not banished to a life in purgatory and they will one day see them again. I realise how blessed I have been having the experiences I've had, as they have helped me deal with my own suicidal thoughts and grief over Dad's death enormously. I believe the time has come to end the stigma associated with suicide. We need to encourage people to be able to speak openly and honestly about their feelings around suicide, rather than having to hide them, like many do, as a dark guilty secret.

Suicide is the leading cause of death among young people aged 20-34 years and for men under 50 in the UK.[i] Someone dies from suicide in the UK every 2 hours and, internationally, I heard that it may even be as frequent as every 43 seconds.

Perhaps, working together, if we can get a life-affirming message out into the world then more suicides could be prevented. If this approach stops just one person from taking the suicide route, then surely it's a message worth sharing.

I know it didn't help my dad and you could argue

that he had no fear of death due to the things I had told him. However, interestingly, since his transition, he has confirmed to me via an incredible medium that he now understands all the stuff I used to talk about and that his soul's journey is never over. He, like everyone else who passes to the other side, has had his life review; it was painful at times, as it is for us all, but he is now continuing to grow and heal in spirit. His role now in spirit is to help others heal who have transitioned via suicide and he wanted to pass on the message that I too would be helping people affected by suicide on the earth plane. This made me smile; dad and daughter now working in partnership to bring about positive, loving and lasting change. What a dream team we are!

I believe the cause of many people's pain stems from an element of low self-esteem, perhaps from childhood and/or challenging life experiences. Traumatised adults often unwittingly create traumatised children and the cycle continues. To break this pattern we need to help *all* children realise how truly special, beautiful, and amazing they are and help them to see that as a reflection in others. We have a duty of care to help them develop healthy and happy hearts, minds, bodies and souls from birth. Education should not be solely focused on academia. It should be more holistic; addressing life skills, creativity, and teaching children how to stay true to our authentic selves.

It is our wish, dream and desire that this book collaboration, written by a group of brave warriors from around the world, will make a significant and positive impact on the lives and souls of those that it reaches.

Every day we will be *#Emerging Proud through Suicide* and will continue to do so until our work here is done!

The more we Love, the more we Care, the more we Share, and together, through the Power of Positivity, we can change the world!

Kelly x

[i]Office for National Statistics 2017 (UK)

*Kelly Michelle Walsh is co-author of the book; 'The Transformative Power of Near-Death Experiences, How the Messages of NDEs Positively Impact the World', with Dr Penny Sartori. All royalties from this book have been pledged to support 'Georgia's Children of the World', a charity aimed at making a positive difference for children affected by poverty and suffering. Find out more about the charity here: https://georgiaschildren. weebly.com*

# A little voice and a listening ear was all it took to turn Pete's life around...

*Pete Cossaboon from Alabama, US, felt like he had nothing left to live for; until a long conversation with an 'Angel' made him realise he had the power to create his own reality. Here Pete tells us his story: from suicidal to Transformation Mentor...*

I had a choice. A very clear and distinct choice. In my right hand was a bottle of Southern Comfort. My left hand had a plastic ziploc bag of four bottles of pills filled with antidepressants and antipsychotics. I already had the CD of my favorite music in the player in my red PT Cruiser sitting in the garage. I was standing in the half stairwell that went from the living room into the garage.

All I had to do was climb into my little car that was always there for me. Just sit down, put the key in the ignition, swallow the pills with the alcohol, and just slowly slip away. All of my problems solved. My suffering and pain that had been present my entire life gone.

But I had a problem. I knew my daughter would be the one to discover my corpse. I couldn't do that to her. I just couldn't. Also, there was a tiny voice. Faint yet persistent, telling me that there was something cool around the corner. The voice kept saying that I was going to miss out on something. Something beyond my current level of comprehension was out there. A collection of moments and experiences like pearls on a strand that would die with me, never having the chance to be alive.

At this point in my life I had lost everything that my ego told me that I was. I was losing my home, I was almost penniless, I had lost my career, I had lost my friends, my wife was divorcing me, and because she could provide a much better life for her, my daughter was with her. I was even about to lose my freedom. There was nothing that I had worked for, nothing that I had used as my definition of me, left.

It was all gone and it was all my fault. I had even lost my own self-respect. I couldn't stand my own reflection in the mirror and had to shave looking out of the side of my eye for six months until I could fully look at my face in the looking glass and see the soul that dwelt inside me. How could I even continue to breathe when the enemy was myself, the me that I needed to take in air for?

I could do it out of love. Love for my daughter, love for the possibilities that that little voice kept telling me were out there. Did I know what those possibilities were? I didn't even have a clue. I couldn't see or imagine anything except for the pain that I was currently in. And I was so tired. So tired of existing. So tired of pretending that everything was okay. Worn out from never letting anyone know what I was going through.

I began my fight for life that night. I called the suicide hotline four times and each time they hung up on me. All I said in my drunken voice was, "I need hope." Then I would hear a dial tone. I slowly typed "suicide help" into my phone and pushed on the number that showed up. A male nurse in some emergency room in some hospital in Tennessee talked to me for almost three hours and helped me to stay alive. I don't know what number I dialed, or who that angel was, but I am here today because he was there for me.

I realized that all of my fears except for one had come true. A few months after this night talking with a new friend, I said almost exactly that to him. He asked me if I knew why and I said no. Then he made a statement that began me on my path to enlightenment. He said, "They came true because you have been focusing on them." A light in my head went off. I realized that I had been placing an order with the Universe by concentrating on all of my fears. I thought that if I could figure out how to deal with my fears I could conquer them. Instead, like a magician, I *conjured* them. I made them true by my attention to them.

From that moment I began my path towards mindfulness. I became aware of the 'me' behind me. I started to open my eyes and see who we truly are, what we truly are, why we are here, and what is possible for us.

Many of those pearls on that strand have revealed themselves to me since that night and they have been beautiful, enchanting, and not at all what I expected. Find a way to survive. Look for someone to help you. Never give up. Things do get better when you allow them to.

*Pete Cossaboon, known as The Angel Encourager, is an Angelic Intuitive Medium. Since 2014, after going through a radical shift in his own personal Spirituality, he has been helping individual clients, a few pets, and groups to tap into the wisdom from the Archangels and transitioned soul energy. His clients have experienced physical, mental, and emotional healing leading to an increase in joy, peace, tranquility, happiness, and all-over wellness.*

*Believing there is so much beyond "The Secret", an avid follower of Abraham Hicks, Tony Robbins, Oprah, Ellen, and so many other teachers, Pete has taken the knowledge and intuition from mentors on this Earthly plain and from the higher realms to bring radical Love to this world. His Spiritual connection combined with his voracious appetite in studying quantum physics and his degree in Mathematics has given him a view of the world that makes his teachings relevant and timely.*

*Believing this world is starving for leaders, he has taken on the role of mentor to teach and heal a world in pain and suffering.*

*Find out more about Pete at: http://petecossaboon.com*

# Ivy learned that sacrificing herself is neither necessary, nor possible

*Artist Ivy from New Jersey on the US east coast has been a voice of HOPE in this community since she #Emerged Proud in the film in 2017. When invited to share her story for the Kinda Proud book series, she said; 'I feel like I could write for all of them', and I guess her voice resonates with the majority; we just can't fit ourselves or our experiences into labels or book title boxes. Here's an artistically portrayed snippet of her journey, which demonstrates a common understanding; that suicidal ideation can come from a deep sense of disconnection...*

I've been killing myself since my first birthday. So I've been told, I screamed my head off until everyone who came to greet me left the house, and only my mom was there. Happy Birthday Ivy.

Not really suicidal, just shy and deep into my soul, harboring something. I remember sitting at the table as a toddler, learning to write my name. It was like I was re-learning who I was, or learning who I was for the first time.

At some point the good memories were overlapped by all the painful ones. My mind became a labyrinth of dark, sad, lonely memories. But one way or another someone(s) or something(s) within or without helped me get by. So what could be described as manic depression, could also be divine intervention.

Losing people I love...losing the connections that held me...that's when I became lost. That's when life seemed 'un-livable'...

I remember praying and hearing nothing, and crying out for my parents in bed. I remember sharing a bed with my siblings, and the fear...we'd keep the blankets around our whole head and only leave a hole big enough to breathe through and see. I remember all the times I swallowed bottles of tylenol, aspirin and other medication to see if I could stop the suffering. It never killed me, it just poisoned Ivy. Funny how that nickname took on new meaning.

Even my art 'poisoned' me, as I touched the solvents

with bare hands and held multiple brushes between my teeth. But it also set me free. The chemicals I've absorbed, the toxicity, the soup my brain rests in...the antibiotics, the pills, the birth control, the SSRI's, the Antipsychotics, did I miss any? Yes...the morphine when I lost my first-born to miscarriage. I have been separated from my body, almost quite literally 'beside myself' for years...quite possibly longer than I know myself.

Have I tried to kill myself? Yes. So many times. Did I want to die? No. But I was going through a spiritual process...I was dying of heartache, I was dying to be reborn, and I needed a connection that wasn't being provided.

Now my body and mind and spirit are a trine. I feel so much and sense so much that I can only hope to slow down enough to remember to breathe. And yet, I am here! I am present. I have not been decapitated. I have not been psychically castrated. I have not had my voice stolen. I have been reborn and I am finding that my family is nearly limitless. Family is a unit and a cluster and extends beyond what I could have ever imagined.

What do I mean by 'family?' I mean that consciousness has changed and I love humanity. I would sacrifice myself for the all, but the lesson I learned was that I am loved and this sacrifice is neither necessary nor possible.

We are strong together.

I hear we are louder together, yes?

We are not alone.

We will not be broken.

I love you.

And now I love me too

*Connect with Ivy here: https://www.facebook.com/ IvyChayaArt*

# His brother's tragic death led Steve to almost take his own life; now he rises strong in support of providing hope to others

*Steve Carr #Emerges Proud to tell the world how the tragic death of his brother Paul led him to finally 'rise like a phoenix from the flames after hitting rock bottom'...*

Friday 13th September 1991, aged just 15 years, my life was changed forever. My dear brother was tragically killed, along with four other children, by a reckless drunk driver in the Akers Way horror crash in Swindon. Paula Barnes, 15, Belinda Brown, 19, Paul Carr, 16, Sheree Lear, 8, and 7-year-old Ian Lilley were playing on the grassed area off Akers Way when the driver lost control of his car at high speed and crashed into the group of youngsters.

The tragedy shook the community and provoked fury among campaigners who had long been calling for a lower speed limit and other safety measures on the road.

I received no support or help following my loss, due to my father's decision that my sister and I would be OK. Instead, I chose to mask the trauma and deep pain with alcohol, cigarettes and drugs.

My mother and father divorced shortly after it happened and I was forced out of my family home.

I lost contact with my mother, father and sister, I could not hold on to any form of relationship for long periods due to the fear of loss and rejection, and as fast as I was gaining friends, jobs and relationships I was losing them.

During my early 30s, things started to look up for me when I managed to hold down a job for long enough to buy a house. But then I found cocaine. I thought I was doing well until I found cocaine, or cocaine found me.

I became an addict in a very short space of time. After a little under a year of taking cocaine, I lost my house, my job, and my friends. I lost everything, and my habit was costing me £100 a day. I couldn't stop what I was doing to myself until one day I pushed it too far.

I became homeless with just enough money for one more high, the last high. With a concoction of drugs and alcohol including cocaine, methadone, and legal highs, I vowed to take my own life.

Something happened that day and I was saved, the concoction almost killed me, but something pulled me back, something saved me.

I can't say what it was but I was given another chance.

After suffering a breakdown due to work related stress, and my employment being terminated whilst off sick, I attempted taking my own life a further two times before I was diagnosed with mental health problems.

Borderline PTSD, High Functioning Anxiety, Depression, Stress, Addiction, Childhood Trauma.

I remember the third suicide attempt quite vividly. I had just taken 24 grams of Methadone, half a gram of strong cocaine, half a litre of Whiskey and half a gram of legal high 'Spice'. I fell back onto my bed and knew I was overdosing and slipping into unconsciousness; it felt quite normal, like I was falling asleep. I felt warm and as if I was floating on water, then a rush came where I was falling backwards. It was then four faces appeared before me.

Two of the four faces I recognised: one was my nan who had sadly passed away 4 years prior to my suicide attempts and the other was my brother.

They both said 'come with us, you'll be safe'. I knew at this point if I did, I would have died. I was fighting death, I was slipping in and out of unconsciousness for eight solid hours, each time falling deeper, but I wouldn't let go. I was petrified, I was sweating, I was delirious, I thought I was going to die and now, after trying to take my life, I didn't want to.

Once I had come through the other side of the overdose, I knew something was different, I had seen death, I had seen my brother, I had seen my nan. I didn't see them in the form of figures, I saw their faces. It was very clear what they said to me, I had experienced the other side.

The other side was dark, like the night sky, but also very calming; there was no drama, no noise, nothing was in the way, all just *was*. It felt like swimming underwater in the sea, or what I imagine being in space felt like with no gravity.

I can still remember it as clear as day, three years later.

The best way I can explain it is like this: you know the moment you drift off into sleep, when your eyes feel heavy and you feel a warm heady sensation course through you just before sleep begins - this is how it felt.

The very next day I gave up smoking after 25 years, I gave up taking drugs after 25 years, and was finally resigned to the fact that I needed professional help.

The night before I asked my brother and asked God for help: I pleaded with them and stated that if they saved me from this hell on earth I was experiencing I would pray every day and go to church as often as I could. I have to say at this point that I was not a practising Christian, or a believer in God for that matter.

There are several influencing factors that helped spark the want in me for change that night. The first is that I had hit rock bottom, I had no friends, I alienated them all to protect them when I found cocaine, as I didn't want them to know about my dirty little secret. The next was that my life had got to the stage where it was well and truly out of control. The third was that I could remember there was a brief time I had everything a 'normal' person could wish for: a house, money in the bank, a car, holidays, friends, and finally I had a belief; I believed that something bigger than myself was, and could help me, first I had to let go of the Ego.

I believe my Ego died that night, I believe I had a spiritual awakening; what I thought was the end of the world was actually the start of a new life, one where I had to find out who I actually was.

There are mixed views on suicide, people will say things like it's selfish, or he/she must have been mad/crazy. That simply isn't the case. Take it from a survivor: the last thing you are is selfish, you actually are putting everybody else before you and that's the problem, you forget about yourself. You want to make everybody else happy; you keep giving and giving until you have nothing left. Your life isn't your own as you are trying to do the best you can with what you have.

My transition to consciousness after the failed suicide attempts was so incredibly painful but now I believe it was necessary.

It was the start of my reawakening and the beginning of my healing journey. Today I am proud to say I am no longer trapped by my past. I chose to confront my demons head on; I chose the path of conscious awareness, self and personal development. I chose to take a look at what was driving me, my subconscious beliefs and to start life from scratch, almost like being reborn. Everything I thought I knew was wrong - it was as if I had been brainwashed from an early age and it wasn't serving me any longer, the battle was far too great, the burden far too heavy. I believe that there is a driving force, an energy behind everything, and it was knowing that there is something bigger than me that saved me that day. I don't believe there to be a god per se, as in a person, I believe that god is a power, and it's in all of us and everything; there is a reason and a purpose for us all.

I feel lucky to be on this journey through life discovering my own true purpose, to have been gifted with another chance, to have seen total despair to be brought back and appreciate life, the small things, and be grateful for living in abundance. I believe we are here just to experience life through our flesh and bones, we are a physical extension of source energy, sent here to live, love, heal and play. Life is as serious or as complicated as we choose to make it, each lived in our own unique way. There is no right or wrong, just what's right for us.

Life is truly amazing. I now have my own Mental Health education business and have recently qualified as a private pilot, I've walked all of Britain and I have the most amazing partner who supports me.

All of this was born out of hitting rock bottom, and I rose like a phoenix from the flames, inspiring and teaching others to do the same.

My brother, Paul Carr 16 yrs old, tragically taken on Friday the 13th of September 1991 in a devastating car accident that rocked the entire community. My purpose and passion were all stemmed from this amazing soul. His memory lives on in my work.

"Change happens when the pain of staying the same is greater than the pain of change."

- Tony Robbins

*Web: www.stevecarr.net and www.mindcanyon.co.uk*

*Twitter: @smcarrs*

*Twitter: @Mindcanyonco*

*Email: connect@stevecarr.net*

# It took a complete suicidal breakdown for Bev to 'TRUST' in the divinity of her Higher Self

*Bev Pirie from Manchester quite literally sunk to rock bottom before she could 'Trust' in her intuitive spiritual wisdom. It took healing herself to train to become the provider of 'messages of love and evidence that we do not die, but simply move on to a state of higher consciousness'.*

*Here, Bev bravely shares her personal journey...*

In February 2011 my world fell apart when a close

friend suddenly passed away. The sense of loss I felt was so profound and I found it almost impossible to function or come to terms with their death. I was already having a difficult time with my own mental health prior to this event, due to ongoing financial issues caused through our home and work. When I thought things couldn't get any worse I was made aware of a potential life-changing revelation which was to impact my marriage. The following week I lost another friend and I literally felt like I was being emotionally swallowed up. I was in shock and I wasn't coping well.

I could see no end to our problems and I could only see grey in everything. I tried so hard to keep going but it became a daily battle between wanting to live and wanting to die. Prior to all these events happening, things had already been very difficult. I had been diagnosed with Hypothyroidism and Myalgic Encephalomyelitis (ME), so my health had declined over the previous 5 years. I believe the constant stress and worries over our financial difficulties compounded things greatly. We had bought our home in 2002; a Victorian Semi, and little did we know it was going to become a monster that was constantly hungry.

I believe the next event was divinely timed to help give us a positive focus and keep me here: our daughter announced she was pregnant in May 2011. She was single and recently returned home. We needed and wanted to support her. The news was an unexpected shock, but we had a moment of happiness followed by a large reality check - the potential financial problems on an already desperate situation.

I tried to push things down and carry on. Our lives changed forever on the 7th December when our grandson was born. He gave us hope and for a short time I was able to put everything behind us.

Unfortunately, things continued to get progressively worse over the next two years; having to cope with ever increasing debt, supporting our family, repairs on our home and the stress of my job resulting in a severe negative effect on my health. I had been trying to support everyone and keep it all together but I finally hit rock bottom and not even the joy of our grandson could help me. It had been almost three years of constant life-changing events which I simply couldn't take anymore.

I felt suicidal and had thoughts of: 'Would I even be missed?'

Everything came to a head in September 2013. Myself and my husband had a horrendous row and I gave him an ultimatum. I can see now it was an emotional breakdown and everything came to the surface in that precise moment. I couldn't carry on, we either had to sell the house or I had to leave before I gave up completely. I was consumed with depression and not even the antidepressants were working.

I'd never felt so lost in all my life; I was so distraught

I walked out of the house with my dog Sky. I was sobbing uncontrollably, the heavens opened and I was drenched to the bone. I found myself in the open field not far from where we lived and sat on the ground sobbing, asking for help. I'd truly had enough, I was beyond lost, I was done, I was broken. I called upon the heavens and shouted:

'Help me God, help me Angels!' I was desperate and needed help. I was in such a dark place that I felt completely alone.

I do have a belief system that there is something greater than us. I was very spiritual but during this period I was totally consumed with depression and lost all faith in the divine.

I pulled myself up off the floor, completely drenched, and saw the most beautiful rainbow in the sky as I heard the word 'TRUST' loudly in my mind. I was unsure if it was my imagination. I walked home in a daze, emotionally drained. I didn't want another row, I was done, but when I arrived home my husband was waiting for me. He took one look at me and said, 'Let's sell!'

We placed our house on the market in late November and sold it in January. We moved into our new home, finally debt-free, and things began to feel more hopeful. In that first year I began to open up more to my own spiritual pathway; so many synchronicities became apparent. I began to see and feel spirit more and I knew that, finally, I could begin to embrace this gift and life.

I'd previously tried hard to ignore it and push it away but, as the weeks passed, I began to understand that my energy and my thoughts were beginning to change. The more I opened my heart, the more alive and joyful I felt.

I started to feel more aligned with life and things became very clear; I have work to do. I have to help bring love and light into our world by helping those who feel lost or are in pain. I can help them through my Spiritual Readings. I was also drawn to be attuned to Usui Reiki so that I could give healing too.

During my meditations I was shown people coming to our home in great sadness and leaving uplifted. I could also help to empower others through workshops and healing circles.

So in 2016 I took a deep breath; a leap of faith you could call it. I created a Facebook page dedicated to my Mediumship and Healing. I submitted it and very quickly I took my first booking for a spiritual reading. In that precise moment I knew my life was going to change. I could not have foreseen how, and in so many unimaginable ways.

I was so inspired and loving the new energy I was receiving. It was wonderful to help so many. Things started to become very busy and I finally made the decision to retire from work so that I could dedicate my life to helping others. I became a Usui Reiki Master/Teacher placing me in a position to help many in the future to be attuned themselves.

Today I work as a full time Spiritual Medium & Healer, bringing messages of love and evidence that we do not die, we simply move on to a state of higher consciousness.

Recently I have been encouraged by my Spiritual team, my guiding voice, to run my own wellbeing retreats for those who are looking to tap into their own abilities; to take time to nurture and step out of life for a little while - allowing themselves to breathe, take stock and enjoy holistic treatments, meditation and mindfulness sessions.

I'm helping others to shine, to create, to believe in the beauty of life through workshops and healing days, and so much more.

I strive every day to be the best version of myself and to show others that you can overcome adversity, no matter how difficult things may be.

I've not experienced any depression or anxiety for almost 4 years since starting my spiritual journey.

The power of positivity is my life force and helps keep me lifted. I continue to shine my light. I have a purpose, a reason to continue on this path until it's my time to go home, where I will carry all my experiences with me.

I heard the word 'TRUST' and I do every day, in a higher loving force.

*Facebook: Bev Pirie (Spiritual Medium)*

*Twitter : @bev_pirie*

*Instagram: Bev_Pirie*

## Dee tells us how a tragedy in her life led to her creating positive change

*Dee from Maidstone in Kent has channelled the pain of her best friend's suicide into campaigning for positive change in social housing law for vulnerable people, and we are Kinda Proud of her for all she has achieved! Dee tells us the tragic story that catalysed her passion...*

So what does 'My Side of Suicide' feel like?

Initially, 18 months ago, it felt 'horrendous'. A rollercoaster of extreme 'highs' and 'lows'. How could I feel 'high' in such a dark time? The answer being the peace I felt 'knowing' my hun was in a better place; his pain was over. This would lift my spirits, though just for a short while, along with the many memories we had made together.

But the 'lows' would soon find me crashing again when I was alone. The very person that most would say was the strongest person they knew, wanting to scream, shout and cry, yet there was so much fear, alongside such powerful emotions. Fearing it may never stop, I would lay motionless on my bed, knowing it was one of those 'wobbly' moments, which would soon subside, yet was so very scarily draining.

So 'My Side of Suicide' 18 months on, is now being written by a different version of me; for no one need tell me I've changed, I feel it every day. This different me finding new ways, strategies, goals to get through each day. For those who die from suicide, their pain is passed on to those loved ones left behind.

So what did 'My Side of Suicide' do?

I joined my local SOBS group; such a blessing connecting with those that 'get' you. I became very aware of various emotions surrounding suicide: loss, guilt and anger being prevalent for others. I can remember people saying to me in the very early days that I would become angry. I felt blessed yet again. No, never!!! Why would I? That's my hun - never a cross word was exchanged in life either.

I started a Campaign, to fill that void that will never quite be filled, for I'd lost my hun, my soul friend.

On reflection, remembering vividly not wanting to be 5 minutes without him, I've come a long way 18 months on, yet there's still a long way to go too. My better days are getting there, my bad days will always remain difficult; there is no doubt of this and it's something I have somewhat resigned myself to.

So I literally threw myself into my Campaign to try to remain focused and bring about change for others. I had little expectations, yet there have been some incredibly overwhelming outcomes, including my hun being at Downing Street, the details of which can be read in the Campaign links below.

### Give Up Your Pets or Your Home?

### (In Loving Memory of John Chadwick)

On March 16th 2017, my world was turned upside down, etched in my heart forever. Since then I made a promise to myself, that I would not just accept this tragedy had happened, by just walking away and saying nothing at all...

My very best friend, my 'hun', John Chadwick, became a victim to suicide on this day, after being forced to choose between homelessness and giving up his beloved pets, Theo, Tinkerbell and their feline best friend Gizmo. I feel it's therefore vital to give some insight into my hun's life and struggles, and certainly how his furbabies had such a positive impact on his mental wellbeing; indeed they were the difference between his life and his death...

My hun was born in Salford, and he eventually walked out of his troubled life some 12 years ago and became street homeless in London for a couple of years. He was found wandering the streets by St Mungo's Homeless Charity. They had assessed he was in a vulnerable state of mind, his physical wellbeing having been affected too. He had become addicted to alcohol to survive living on the streets and to get through each day. St Mungo's placed my hun into their care and later transferred him to a detox unit in Kent. From there, my hun was transferred to Kenward Trust, in Yalding, Kent, in 2007 - a Drug and Alcohol Rehab. He completed a 6 month rehabilitation programme and later secured a tenancy with a private landlord in Maidstone, Kent.

I met my hun in 2008 and was so inspired by his story, I too became employed by Kenward Trust in 2010, and continue to work for them to date.

So my journey with my hun had begun. Little did I realise the full impact of this until after his tragic death...

In 2009, my hun walked back into his life in Salford as his father had become ill. On his return to Maidstone, those old feelings he thought he had faced in therapy came back and he relapsed heavily. He was detoxed and returned back to the community some 2 weeks later. My hun had left the gay clubbing scenes behind him in Manchester, and as I felt he needed a purpose, I got him a kitten called Gizmo. A couple of years later he acquired Theo and Tinkerbell, 2 Jack Russell cross puppies, and his family was complete; they were his furbabies.

My hun had a small close network of friends here in Maidstone, and would accompany my family for Christmas Dinner; he was part of our family. I was always aware that his mental health issues presented as a 'quiet' condition. No one would ever really know just by speaking with him. He was a gentle and kind man and one of the most grounded people I knew; our 9 year friendship was so consistent. He was loved and respected by all who knew him.

The unconditional bond he had with his furbabies: Theo, Tinkerbell and Gizmo, I cannot fully describe as it wouldn't do it justice. When I reflect upon the memories no one can take from me, tears well up instantly. His furbabies absolutely adored him as much as he did them; an unconditional love that cannot be fully expressed unless you had been there to experience it. When I say we as his friends were not enough for my hun, it's no reflection on us as people, my hun loved us all dearly, there is no doubt in my mind of this…but his furbabies were his everything…

My hun was later served with a section 21 at Christmas 2016, as the private landlord wanted to sell up. I knew then this wouldn't end well. Having worked in a housing related role, I knew he wouldn't be able to take his furbabies to temporary accommodation and that it was highly unlikely a permanent tenancy would allow them either. He was evicted on March 6th 2017 and after a meeting with the council he was placed in B & B. That was the last time my hun saw his furbabies and his mental wellbeing deteriorated rapidly.

He was quickly offered a flat by the council on the 7th floor and where animals were not allowed. Their so called duty of care was to house him, without looking at the bigger picture and the evidence provided regarding his previous homeless issues, addiction and the therapeutic benefits his furbabies gave him. He needed them to wake up to and go home to at the end of each day. They gave him a routine, were a great source of comfort, and impacted positively on his mental wellbeing. I advised the council that he wouldn't survive without them. Theo and Tinkerbell had become distraught without him and they were also separated from their feline best friend Gizmo.

On March 16th 2017, my hun took a fatal overdose of prescription medication and alcohol at the B &B, after sending a goodbye text to myself and his best friend Shane, who was caring for Theo and Tinkerbell. My hun told us he loved us and would wait for us. This was also the anniversary of his mother's passing, someone he loved dearly.

I later started a Campaign calling for a Positive Pet

Policy in Housing. I remembered thinking after my hun's death: 'what he's dead and that's that??!! Am I supposed to just walk away now?'

My campaign is not to proportion blame, it will not change what's happened. But by keeping my hun's memory alive, his tragic story may help prevent this happening again, becoming part of a much-needed change for all. Suicide/mental health is a very misunderstood subject, one which many avoid discussing, therefore leaving those who suffer to do so in silence. Pets are proven to have therapeutic benefits, impacting positively on physical and mental wellbeing, particularly for those deemed as vulnerable, alone or homeless.

Since the Campaign really started to take off towards the end of 2017, I have been truly overwhelmed by not only the response from the public, but various organisations and the media alike, who have assisted with pushing the Campaign forwards.

In July 2018 a new Pet Policy was implemented by my local Council as a direct result of my hun's tragic death and my campaign. Those who are now facing homelessness are able to take their pets with them to temporary accommodation if the properties are suitable to do so. However, in terms of more long term tenancies being offered with pets by Private and Social Housing Landlords, my local Council's hands would still remain somewhat tied.

But, I will continue to Campaign for other areas to

make changes to their Pet Policies. I'm aware this is no easy feat and there is no miracle around the corner, but I do feel truly blessed that the change was first implemented with us here in Maidstone, where my hun's life ended.

Please help me campaign to other areas by signing the petition link below and circulating both this and the New Pet Policy News Link to continue keeping this important message out there: that pets are a vital source of wellbeing for many and are part of the family.

Petition Link:
https://www.change.org/p/helen-grant-mp-introduce-pets-as-support-systems-for-the-more-vulnerable-members-of-society/u/21955552

New Pet Policy :
https://www.kentonline.co.uk/maidstone/news/pet-owners-suicide-leads-to-policy-change-186708

About me:
I have worked in Social Care since I was 18. I have two daughters and 4 grandchildren.

I have been a Drug and Alcohol Worker with Kenward Trust, Yalding, Kent since December 2010.

Theo & Tinkerbell are rehomed together and their feline best friend Gizmo is with my daughter.

**Bobbi has used her trauma as a catalyst for positive change; "I want my pain to have a purpose; my mess to have a message."**

*The wisdom Bobbi's gained through such horrific circumstances, speaks to the resilience of the human spirit. Bobbi so rightly talks about how, when we don't deal with 'trauma imprints' of life, the pressure of repressing them leads to 'soul- tiredness'. As Bobbi states: "…grief is a raging river; you have to get into it and let it flow all around you, rather than fighting the current which will suck you under." Once we surrender to it, that can be the*

*beginning of 'soul- thriving'… Accepting help from others isn't weakness; it is only then we have the capacity to truly give from our heart*

On January 25, 2015 my life, my "reality" as I knew it, ended when my husband of 15 years completed suicide, in the driveway of our home. We had an argument that fateful night and, had I known the outcome, I would have changed so many words/actions/choices; not in that I think I could have changed the outcome, but just so I could have more peace surrounding our last words to each other. In the end, the horrific reality of a suicide is that you cannot just apologize, hug it out, or ask for a "do over"; it is an absolute finality and that person forever gets the "last word." There are details I feel need to be shared for one to understand the depth and complexity of our loss and my passion and mission to spread awareness about grief, complicated grief and suicide. However, by the same token, I choose to leave out a lot of the graphic details out of respect for my children and my late husband.

During our argument, Ken went into our master bedroom closet and grabbed our handgun that had been stored in a lock box for years and never loaded (so I thought); a struggle ensued — half of me not believing he was really going to do anything with the gun, thinking it was a manipulation tactic — and the other half of me terrified about what was transpiring. Ken overpowered me and made his way to leave out our back door to the garage and into his car. I begged him to not go and threatened to call the police; this only angered him more. I followed him to the garage and tried to grab the gun away from him as he entered his car. As I grabbed for the gun, I heard a voice, from out of nowhere (I know and believe it to be my Guardian Angel) tell me to "drop the gun and back away." I did drop the gun as Ken backed the car up, backing over my foot, yelling that he would "do it in front of me and the kids if I didn't let him leave." As I ran back into our house to find my cell phone to call 9-1-1, I heard the gunshot. I ran out to find Ken, in the front seat of his car with a single gunshot wound through his chin, and barely breathing. In the midst of the chaos that ensued, my then 7 year-old slipped out of the house and saw his dad in the car. It haunts me still to this day that I was not able to protect my youngest son from that horrific scene. My youngest was shortly thereafter diagnosed with PTSD. What my son and myself witnessed that night compares closely to the true life crimes you watch on television.

The fallout of Ken's decision to complete suicide was incomprehensible; brutal, gut-wrenching and horrific. Ken's family blamed me. They chose to believe Ken's words spoken to one of his sisters, in a phone conversation just hours before Ken took his life, as "truth" and there were a lot of rumors spread by the family that were not remotely ever the truth. Ken was not in his right mind, clearly, and yet, his sister chose to make assumptions on things she knew nothing about. I now know what it feels like to be wrongly accused of murder.

For two weeks I could not close my eyes to sleep; flashbacks haunted me and my heart would not stop racing. I was crawling out of my own skin as PTSD set in and anxiety like I had never known threatened to take my sanity. The only way I was able to close my eyes and get any sleep would be when I would call out to my God and beg him to keep me from going crazy and leaving my boys. Psalm 23 would readily be recited to me each time, from somewhere within me:-

The Lord is my shepherd, I lack nothing. He makes me lie down in green pastures, He leads me beside quiet waters, He refreshes my soul. He guides me along the right paths for His name's sake. Even though I walk through the darkest valley, I will fear no evil, for You are with me; Your rod and Your staff, they comfort me. You prepare a table before me in the presence of my enemies. You anoint my head with oil; my cup overflows. Surely Your goodness and love will follow me, all the days of my life, and I will dwell in the house of the Lord Forever.

In order to understand my journey more fully, I feel it is important to explain a little more about me; my traumatic childhood and my spiritual foundation. I do believe we are given certain trials and struggles in life that "prepare" us to endure our greatest struggles that can, with faith and mercy, become our greatest lessons and, even, blessings.

First, and most importantly, I am a mother to three amazing, resilient, brilliant young men who bless me daily and are the reason I choose to not only survive, but thrive. Namely, Chase (22); Dawson (14); and Dylan (12). I have had a "million" careers in my short lifetime, ranging from college for radiology technology; massage therapy/kinesiology; church secretary; legal secretary/paralegal for 15 years; parapro teacher (Title 1) for several years; and fitness franchisee owner of Jazzercise, Inc., for 11 years.

I was born in Las Vegas, Nevada in March, 1971. I am the youngest of two daughters born to my mother, Jane, and my father, Robert. My mother and father divorced when I was two years old. My mother subsequently became an alcoholic. My sister became more of a mother figure to me, scrounging for food and trying to make sure we ate and survived while my mother was intoxicated 24/7. First trauma "imprint."

My father died of a massive heart attack when I was 11 years old. I remember the viewing of my father in his open casket very vividly and now realize how traumatizing that was. I had not been allowed to have a relationship with him up until about one year prior to his death; I had finally felt like I had a dad and was just getting to know him. I now realize this was my first experience of suppressed grief due to my having to comfort my mother through her grief over the loss of my father, versus her comforting me through my loss. Second trauma "imprint."

My first exposure to suicide came in my mid-30s when I was notified that my childhood best friend,

Nicole, had completed suicide. Her young daughters found her lifeless body hanging in the garage upon returning home from school. I was completely and utterly shocked and never really did process it all completely; realizing this now only after losing my husband to suicide. Third trauma "imprint."

Ken and I suffered four miscarriages in-between my son, Chase, and my son, Dawson. One was a tubal pregnancy. (I'm actually a case study at the University of Oregon for the largest, thriving tubal pregnancy that did not kill the mother.) Having emergency surgery to remove my thriving baby to save my life was very traumatic. Fourth trauma "imprint."

Fast forward to approximately 4 years prior to my husband completing suicide, my mother unexpectedly died after what was to be a short visit to the ER for unexplained stomach pain. She coded and was gone before I could catch a flight to be by her side. Fifth trauma "imprint."

Just one year prior to Ken dying, his father passed away from heart disease. Ken was at his side at the time of his death. I took it very hard as I felt like Ken's dad, Neal, had been like a father figure to me and was the only grandfather my boys had. Sixth trauma "imprint."

Just four months prior to Ken dying, our family dog, Bella, was violently mauled to death by our neighbor's dogs, in front of my youngest son. Seventh trauma "imprint."

Following these losses and, specifically, my mother's death, I started to really evaluate my life; I was soul-tired. I had been raising young kids, working in the schools, running my fitness franchise business and taking care of everything at home so my husband could focus on his career and climb to the top to achieve his status as the youngest employee to make "partner." I was on a quest to find the true, authentic me; what made me happy — an urgency to understand my higher purpose and my God/Universe/Energy at a deeper level.

It is interesting when you start to soul search and ask/pray for help from your higher source; it shakes everything up and it can become a very tumultuous time. It was as if my energy had shifted and I was consumed with wanting to understand how all life worked and how I could better my life and the lives of others. I remember being on a long run, calling out to my God saying "I feel so alone; I don't have a 'community.'" Little did I know how the universe would quickly show me how wrong I was in that belief, just months later.

When Ken died, my "community" surrounded me and my boys. The "community" I did not think I had. It was not his family; it was not even the friends who I thought would be by my side; it was people whose lives I had touched by my work as a volunteer in the schools and, subsequently, my work as a Title 1 Teacher in our school district; it was my customers from my fitness classes; it was strangers and "acquaintances" who would later become some of my closest friends; it was neighbors whom I had known and talked to regularly, but also neighbors whom I had never spoken to. This "community" fed me and my boys with meals for three straight months after Ken died. They regularly took shifts to stay with me at night in those first few weeks. They offered to help with bills and errands and took my boys out to do fun and light-hearted activities. Even my teacher community gave us the monies that had been set aside for the new playground equipment at the elementary school! (Those monies have since been donated back to the school, in remembrance of Ken.)

Even though I had my community's support, I felt completely and utterly alone in my struggles to come to grips with the new reality that was my life. My boys were traumatized and my youngest was in the throws of his own PTSD from the events of that night. I was unable to grieve openly because it would trigger my boys' angst and fear of abandonment; my boys thought I, too, would leave them if I showed any kind of sadness or tears or weariness.

Ken was a great provider. We had a large house in Michigan, as well as a cottage up North with lots of ATVs, a boat, motorcycle and all kinds of "toys" and provisions. These are all great except when you die and cannot take them with you; you leave a lot of property behind for your loved ones to deal with. The paperwork and tasks were un-ending and amidst all of it, I was tried and convicted by members of Ken's family who were busy blaming me for his death and were not supportive of my decisions to rid myself of our family home and other property.

The horrific tragedy engulfed me; I knew I was going to suffocate if I stayed in Michigan. There's that announcement when you are flying when the flight attendants talk about the oxygen mask that drops from above in case of loss of cabin pressure — that was me! I had to put on my "oxygen mask" first if I was going to assist my children. The decision to leave my friends, my work and my community that I had worked so hard to build, was a difficult one. I had tremendous guilt pulling my children from their friends, their schools and their community in their greatest time of loss but I knew if I did not I would not survive. I had to get away from that house; I had to get away from the "sad stares" of my community and friends; I had to get us where we could "start over" and not have every place, restaurant, friendship, encounter, street sign, etc., throw us into memories of what was a life that no longer was. I moved to Texas, not knowing a soul, except having two cousins whom I knew growing up but had not been in contact with since high school. To this date, I am amazed at my ability to be cognizant enough to research, buy a home, and move and establish a thriving life in Texas, just six months following Ken's suicide. This I know for sure was by God's grace.

I commonly compare the aftermath of suicide to the aftermath of a grenade; it spreads shrapnel for miles, injuring and killing countless souls. I call it the "ripple effect." The ripple effects of losing a loved one to suicide are long-standing. Even three years later, I continue to be informed of its effects (some good, some bad) on those who were an integral part of our lives; the heartbreaking reality of suicide — those left behind.

I would say there is a type of "duality" in death; it's either a "gift" that allows us to re-evaluate our lives for the better and allows one to search out its lessons; or you allow it to swallow you into its darkness. I often say that grief is a raging river; you have to get into it and let it flow all around you, rather than fighting the current which will suck you under.

I have chosen to take my experiences as a young suicide widow and give them a purpose. From the massive outpouring my community provided to me and my boys rose my conviction to serve and honor young widows so that they, too, would feel less alone. From a biblical standpoint, we are all called to serve widows.

In my own struggles to reach out and be vocal about my grief and the effects of suicide, I found there were not many resources that fit my trauma and loss. Truth is, not many grief programs specifically deal with young widows and the complexities we face; typically the late spouse being the breadwinner of the family while the woman stays home to raise the family, or works less to support her husband's career. There are many struggles and a stigma that alienates many young widows and, even more so, young suicide widows.

In February, 2018, I founded my non-profit *Widow's Wish* and its community of "Widow Thrive." I want my pain to have a purpose; my mess to have a message. It is also my goal to launch a consulting company that assists businesses and schools regarding suicide and complicated loss, as well as becoming a published author and motivational speaker.

You can choose to THRIVE even in the midst of incredible loss and trauma.

### Bobbi Mason Biography:

Following the loss of my husband in January, 2015, I quickly realized the lack of resources available to young widows and felt an urgency to become an ambassador to young widows and those who have suffered traumatic loss. In February, 2018, I launched Widow Thrive, and the 501(c)(3) non-profit, Widow's Wish Foundation. Through Widow's Wish Foundation https://widowthrive.com/ and my online Facebook Widow Thrive Community https://www.facebook.com/psalm23widow/, I assist and support young widows with the enormous grief "dynamics" that they face, specifically in their first year of loss. Widow's Wish Foundation supplies financial assistance in the form of meals, gift cards for gas, groceries; hosting fundraising events for families; and a Christmas gifting program. I also organize a Houston Widows & Widowers meetup group that encourages local widows/widowers to connect and share their grieving journeys with one another in a casual, fun atmosphere, at various venues once a month.

It is my desire to spread awareness, globally, to the plight of the young widow, the homeless young widows and their children, and the epidemic of suicide and the exponential growing population of suicide widows. I am currently working on two book manuscripts and aspire to collaborate with Oprah, Gabrielle Bernstein and Michelle Steinke-Baumgard.

**Andy from Massachusetts, US, realised that everything could be healed, but only once he was willing to be healed. The bravest thing he did was to be open to asking for, and receiving, help and support.**

*Andy used to live a life of hiding his true feelings; this only spiralled him further into depression and unable to experience real joy in his life. Now a self- confessed 'lover-of-life', Andy uses his life experience to inspire others, including founding; Real Men Feel, a movement encouraging men to accept and express all of their*

*emotions. Andy knows from experience that the strongest thing we can do is admit when we need help; this was the turning point in his inspiring personal story.....*

Life sucks, then you die.

That was my worldview for a long time. When I was 17, I had a pin in my car with that saying on it, in case I needed a reminder.

I didn't need a reminder. I was sure that the world wasn't a safe place. I was confident that I was broken beyond any hope of repair, and that life sucked no matter what I did from a very young age.

My parents were full-time college students when they had me. They got married and tried their best, but they divorced when I was five-years-old. We moved around often in those early years. I was an only child, heavy and shy. Around the same time my dad left our home, a neighbor began molesting me. I knew it was wrong but was afraid if I told anyone, I'd be kicked out of my home too. I stayed quiet and grew even quieter in life.

On the first day of school for the 3rd grade I was sitting on the bus next to one of my few close friends, and I started crying. I had no idea why. I couldn't explain it, I felt sad and scared, even though this was the same school I'd been at for the last two years. This was the moment I recall deciding that I was different. I was broken. I felt things other people didn't, and it was wrong.

For years I hid my depression and suicidal thoughts. I knew I wouldn't live long. Other people would talk about what they wanted to be when they grew up, I had no interest in growing. My dad often said high school is the best years of your life, so I decided it would be foolish to bother living beyond them.

Sometimes I couldn't even wait that long. My first attempt to end my life came when I was 13, and 15, 16, 17, 18…you get the picture.

It took me multiple "failed" suicide attempts before I allowed myself to ponder that maybe, just maybe, there is a better way. I obviously wasn't good at ending my life so there must be a better way to navigate my life. Things began to change when I allowed for the possibility that just maybe I was supposed to be here.

I was 23 the last time I was in a mental health hospital. It was the first time I put myself into a hospital and I did so before making any suicide attempt. I felt like such a grown-up. I'd finally realized I could ask for and receive help without resorting to self-harm. I didn't need to try and end my life as my only means to change it.

Each decade of my life has been better than the prior one. Suicidal thoughts still showed up, and perhaps always will when I'm under emotional stress, but attempts ended and actions and plans have been rarer each decade too.

Today, I love life and even more surprising is that

I know life loves me. In my thirties, I embraced personal growth and creating a positive mindset. Some people I meet think I'm so happy, they don't believe it when I tell them about my suicidal background. I began sharing my story so people could know that depression and suicidal thoughts don't have to last your entire life. Everything can be healed, but only once we are willing to be healed. We need to be open to asking for and receiving help and support.

Life doesn't suck. I find that life gets better and better. When I was a kid, the only place I heard anyone talk about suicide was in a mental health hospital. I'm out to change that.

The reason I'm here is to enjoy life and to remind people they can enjoy it too. Life can be heaven or hell, the power is in our choices. Choose wisely, my friend.

**"Sometimes we need to learn the same lesson repeatedly to truly integrate it into our being. In such cases it isn't really the same lesson; it is deeper levels of the lesson" Andy**

**Andy Grant Bio:**

I am a best-selling author, award-winning speaker, Transformational Energy Coach, Akashic Records Reader, and Life Activation Practitioner.

I am also the founder of Real Men Feel, a movement encouraging men to accept and express all of their emotions. I have been producing and hosting the Real Men Feel podcast since February 2016.

As a survivor of multiple suicide attempts, I know how low we as human beings can feel, and I am committed to helping people realize how magnificent life is meant to be. My Amazon best-seller, "Still Here: How to Succeed in Life After Failing at Suicide", is a book that has helped people around the globe, and includes everything I wished I knew at a younger age. I am also a lead editor and contributor at the Good Men Project: GoodMenProject.com.

*Learn more at TheAndyGrant.com.*

*Connect with Andy on Facebook: facebook.com/ AndyGrantLoveYourLife/*

*Twitter: @navitascoaching*
*@realmenfeelorg*

*Instagram: @andy_grant*

*LinkedIn: https://www.linkedin.com/in/ andrewfgrant/*

**Katherine, from Australia, quite rightly says: 'this word 'suicide' is not something to be feared, rather one that we could understand more deeply.'**

*Katherine Baldwin-Thomson is Kinda Proud of what she's achieved due to her personal healing journey, and we are Kinda Proud of her for sharing her story with us! Here Katherine tells us how she went from using alcohol to numb her pain, to helping others to find the light at the end of their dark tunnel...*

My name is Katherine and I am 44 years of age. Looking back at myself as a child, I was very sensitive and quiet. I was spiritual and creative from a young age and liked to be in my own world – not much has changed there. Like many other people my childhood was varied with a mixture of experiences. I had some great times being raised by my loving parents, but I also had some deeply traumatic experiences. We were poor and my parents often needed to work two jobs, so I had very little choice but to stay with my grandparents, who were mentally ill.

When you are a young child and you have been physically and mentally abused it does leave scars and pain that can manifest later in life. Pain that we attempt to cover up in order to cope.

I didn't have a good relationship with my grandparents to say the least. I will never forget the smell of falling asleep on musty shag carpet under my nan's king size bed to avoid being beaten by her with a wooden broom handle. However, throughout my life I have always known that I was not what was happening to me, but rather part of something greater – as we all are.

To cope with some of the trauma from my early life of staying with my grandparents, I started drinking when I was 14 years of age. It was the only way that I felt I could numb my pain at the time. Then, the years went by and I had been drunk and passed out more times than I care to remember.

When I turned twenty I decided that it was time to get my life in order and had the opportunity to open my own shop. The shop was called the Purple Angel and the business was a dream come true for me as I loved working for myself. The business did very well and I was really finding my feet. For the third year in a row we were making a profit and I was so happy that I was finally doing what I wanted.

Then one day, my mum, who is a huge inspiration to me and a loving support in my life, told me she had a brain tumour and that the doctors were unsure if she would survive the surgery. My dad ran a supermarket and had to support my mum. We lived in the country and did not have the option for home-nursing and the level of care my mum would need. She required round the clock medication and needed help feeding, bathing and dressing. I decided the right thing to do was to close my business and look after my mum day and night, a decision I would never regret. This was a task of many highs and lows and there was an immense amount of pressure placed on me at the age of 23.

A year and a half later my mum had recovered well enough to not need my care anymore. I then needed to find work and moved to Melbourne as there were more work opportunities than in the country. I took the first job that I had an interview for and started working at a supermarket. My boyfriend and I upsized our home and we were now living in a large house with our dog Wilbur and our cat Chocolate. To many this would have been the ideal stepping stone, however I started to feel overwhelmed and under pressure. I was dealing with the emotional struggle of losing my business, seeing my mum sick for so long, and the heartache that came with all of that.

I was constantly worried that my mum would need me and being so far away from her kept me in a state of constant stress. I remember it all getting too much for me. I was starting to feel deeply depressed with the weight of the world on my shoulders. I felt like I was trapped and that no one would understand how I was feeling. During that time all my childhood trauma and abuse surfaced and I started drinking again. I was in overwhelm and feared that I had nowhere to turn.

One particular day, I recall my thoughts racing through my head, my heart pounding and my breath being short and shallow. It was at this point that I started to think that maybe everyone would be better off if I wasn't there. I would be better, all the pain would cease and all the pressure in my head would finally stop! There would be silence and I would be free.

The idea of silence and no pain felt so good. So I got up off the ground and went to the kitchen and got the sharpest knife and a towel. I placed the knife on my wrist and began to push the blade into the veins. Just at that time my partner unlocked the front door and ran over to me when he heard me sobbing and saw what I was doing. He shouted 'what are you doing!?' I dropped the knife and broke down. It was at that moment I was so grateful he had come home and stopped me. It was also at that point that I knew I didn't want to kill myself. I just wanted the pain, fear and overwhelm to go away. I just wanted to see a light at the end of the tunnel. I needed to feel that I wasn't alone and that everything was going to be okay. I wanted to be held and understood.

I went to see someone about how I was feeling. In just four sessions of talking about how I felt and being given simple coping tools, I was back on my feet and feeling like I could cope again. I just needed to start healing the hurt I had gone through as a child and a teenager. I knew that in healing myself and learning to be kind to myself and forgiving myself, I would be in a better position to forgive and let go of those who had hurt me in the past. I also had a sense that it would give me insight and the skills to help other people to do the same.

That is why it makes me very proud to say that at the age of 44 I have been a healer and counsellor for over 20 years and I have been a Vortex Subconscious specialist for over 13 years now. What this means is that I help people remove old subconscious beliefs and blocks that are held within their subconscious patterning. I specialise in helping children overcome trauma and help women to get back on their feet after difficult times. I help people live their best life possible.

I started doing this work because of my own journey

and wanted people to know that they had somewhere to turn when they were down. My desire was to help people come out of stress and overwhelm just like I did and begin to thrive again.

When you really think about it, this word 'suicide' is not something to be feared, rather one that we could understand more deeply. When we understand that the person is feeling lost, overwhelmed and like they have nowhere to turn, we also understand that all they are really reaching for is a lifeline of love – a helping hand to let them know that everything is going to be alright.

**Katherine's bio:-**

I am the CEO and Founder of Angel Soul Healing; Channel and Healer of The Vortex Subconscious Healing Modality; Owner and Manager of The Angel Soul Healing School and Center.

I am an Advanced Master in The Vortex Subconscious Sound Healing, Subconscious Specialist, Reiki Master, Shaman Master, Advanced Multi-Dimensional Soul healer, Pallowah Practitioner, Trance Channel Master and Doreen Virtue Realm worker. I purely channel with Jesus, Kuan Yin, The Archangels of the universe, Uluru, pure source and so many more.

I Channelled my own healing Modality, The Vortex

Subconscious Sound Healing. I am the Inventor of the I AM Happy Stick; The artist and producer of the I AM, Empowerment Oracle Card Deck for women, kids and men. I have been a public speaker and performer for almost 13 years.

I now dedicate my life to helping my clients rebuild their lives.

Contact me via my website:
https://angelsoulhealing.com.au

# Artist Joe from Oregon, USA, is Kinda Proud of being a 'Survivor'

*We are Kinda Proud of Joe for allowing himself to 'feel all the feels' and work through and communicate his emotions; for speaking up about his experiences to end the stigma of suicide and to encourage others to open up. Being that vulnerable takes a lot of bravery, and Joe is right, it's the only way we make these kind of experiences an acceptable conversation topic for others. The more of us that speak out, we hope that less people will suffer in silence.*

*Here's why Joe describes himself as a 'Survivor' in his own words...*

When asked who I am, rather than speak based on years of fear and poor self-talk, I choose to say "I am a survivor."

I SURVIVED a childhood living in a filthy house with not a lot of money, sometimes eating nothing but Mac & Cheese and hot dogs for a week at a time just to get by. My mom was not very good at taking care of the home and family back then and my dad was very disconnected and did not show affection at all. My parents would fight and argue daily, and it would all get worse around the age of 14 when my dad was involved in a truck accident that left him with a broken neck and unable to work.

I SURVIVED being sexually assaulted on more than one occasion at the age of seven years old by our male babysitter.

I SURVIVED being physically assaulted by a man on my 18th birthday that put me in the hospital after I bumped the antenna on his car as I walked by with friends.

I SURVIVED being rear-ended by a semi-truck whilst parked in traffic on a freeway.

I SURVIVED the loss of my three-day old daughter and would be divorced from her mom within weeks after her death. All of this left me devastated as all

I wanted more than anything was to be a good dad and a good husband.

I SURVIVED a two-year period of destructive behavior following my daughter's death that included a speeding ticket for 144-mph in a 55-mph, being drunk almost every night of the week and some days, doing dumb things on a skateboard and motorcycle as I felt I had nothing to lose.

I SURVIVED a skateboard fall that would leave me permanently disabled followed by more than a dozen surgeries to my arms just to get back some use of my hands.

I SURVIVED a second marriage that was very unhealthy for the both of us as well as our three kids and ended in a messy divorce and custody battle.

I SURVIVED a house fire that would destroy my home and the fire report said occupant was less than 30 seconds from not exiting the house.

I SURVIVED an 85-mph head on collision with a drunk driver that left me with no memory before the age of 11, a severe head injury, and more surgeries to my arms causing more issues for my disability.

I SURVIVED what I like to call the church trap where I fully devoted my life to Jesus Christ, worked at the church, went to bible college, and volunteered with youth until I realized the choices being made by my church, my wife at the time, my bible college, and our head pastor in no way lined up with what I was reading about Jesus in the bible.

I SURVIVED being t-boned by two high school girls that blew through a stop sign totaling my truck.

I SURVIVED a mental breakdown following my second divorce that sent me to a facility for a couple of weeks, twice.

I SURVIVED seven years of being a single dad to three beautiful and amazing kids while doing my absolute best to be a positive role model, and giving them a better upbringing than I had as a child, regardless of our situation. I have always put their needs before my own.

I SURVIVED the financial mess that my divorce to my kids' mother left me in and with no choice but to file bankruptcy on all the things that had already been taken from me in our divorce years earlier.

I SURVIVED the loss of my grandmother after three years of helping my mom take care of her as Alzheimer's and dementia ate away at her mind.

I SURVIVED being run over by an SUV while snow blowing a driveway, by a lady who was not looking in her rearview mirror.

I SURVIVED, most recently, a double disk replacement surgery in my neck that was caused by degenerated disks that happened because of my disability.

I SURVIVED PTSD, and so many thoughts of SUICIDE over the years, that I literally lost count. I had never shared any of my dark thoughts with anyone over the years, until recently after 18 months of going to an amazing counselor and recently losing yet another friend to suicide. I decided it was time to be honest with myself and those around me about my struggle with suicide!

After well over a year of going to my counselor, it finally clicked for me that my past does not define me, my fears do not define me, the horrendous things I've been through do not define me, my hurts do not define me, my disabilities do not define me.

What defines me is the fact that I am a survivor; I am still here, and my recent understanding that life isn't out to get me. I am a great father, I've raised three loving and hardworking kids; I'm a great husband to my now wife of three years; I'm a great son and friend; I'm an Artist that makes beautiful creations from jewelry to large scale art installations that are known worldwide. I'm a healer that can speak with so many different people, as I've most likely walked the path you're on at one point in my life.

A counselor once told me "You have been through more things than any ten people you could gather off the street and you're still here and you're still going, there is a bigger plan for your life young man."

What keeps me going? What has helped me finally find my way out of that dark place?

Lots of love!

I am working on self-care, learning to love and take care of myself, learning to breathe, learning who I am, learning and understanding how I work so I can grow, and doing it all with so much love and support from my kids, my wife, my mom and dad, and my counselor.

I'm honestly quite amazed at how easy some things are and yet how hard other things are regarding my personal journey.

I can say for the first time in my life, the only time suicide crosses my mind is when I'm trying to think of ways to speak up and end the stigma around suicide that kept me from asking for or seeking help so many times in my life.

Don't get me wrong, there are still days that are very hard — days that I have doubts, days I fall back into old thought patterns, and even panic attacks that can last for days. The difference is I'm learning to be 'in the moment' and feel all the feels while trying to work through and communicate why I'm feeling these things, rather than let my fears take control.

I am, for the first time in my 43 years, in a place where I can see the beauty that life has to offer while still honoring the struggles and trials I've been through in life that have made me who I am today.

Joe Beal


*To find out more about Joe and his art work go to:*
*www.nostalgicmetal.com*

# Abbie is KindaProud of how she's become a 'Warrior'

*As Abbie learned, keeping our pain inside and putting on a front only serves to direct our pain inwards and can often lead to self-destructive behaviour, like self-harm. By speaking out about our struggles and normalising them we don't know who we will positively impact and inspire...knowing that we are not alone in our pain can be the key to turning things around. Abbie now uses her own journey through the darkness to inspire hope for young people in Norfolk, UK and beyond, in the same way that she was inspired to change her life by an idol*

For as long as I can remember I wanted my life to end. That was until I discovered an unlikely hero in the form of a pop star that changed my life forever. Growing up I'd always felt out of place, as if I was surviving instead of living. I don't really know when I started feeling depressed and unhappy with every aspect of my appearance, it's almost as if it was a constant state of mind, so much that I just thought that was normal and how my brain was going to be forever. I soon thought that there was only one way out.

It seemed to everyone around me that life was good. I was just a normal kid, excited to see what I could do with my life. No one saw the signs, no one saw the constant battle I was having with myself about the way I looked. I never felt comfortable in my skin, looking at magazines and seeing these beautiful women wondering why my body was so different, not knowing they'd been photoshopped. I guess it was only a matter of time before the rollercoaster that was my life would make me sicker.

My life only got harder when I was in high school: I was bullied for everything I did and didn't do, to the point that teachers would laugh along with the students. I was going further into the black hole that I'd always envisioned ending up in. By the time I was 15 I'd had people threatening me, telling me to kill myself or they'd do it for me. I felt unwanted everywhere, I had nowhere to be safe.

I turned on myself rather quickly, thinking that there clearly must be something wrong with me if everyone else thought so. I don't know where I got the idea of self-harm from, but it soon became my addiction. It started with a rubber band on my wrist. When that wouldn't satisfy my need for control, I turned to more serious methods, ruining my arms and my legs. I felt like my life was completely spiralling and I was getting closer to the final stage. I couldn't leave my house without my brain being directed to things I could jump off or in front of. This continued to be my life until, at the age of 18, something, or should I say someone, came along and changed everything.

Mid-January 2014, it was just like any other day. I was sitting in my mum's car, the radio was on, my mood was in a good but, normal for me, depressed state. The next song started: some beautiful piano riffs - it was a song I'd heard before but this time it was like hearing the words and the message for the first time. Those piano riffs belonged to Demi Lovato's song *Skyscraper*. At that moment I started to cry, hiding it of course from my mum who had no idea of what I was feeling nor what was happening in my life.

Later on, at home, I was feeling terrible. I was about to go to my normal 'feel-better' coping mechanism, which of course actually only gave me a few seconds of relief before I felt horrible again, but for some reason those few seconds seemed worth it. Something clicked in my brain at that moment, I wanted to get through that night better than before. I searched for the very song that had given me goose-bumps earlier that day: once again those wonderful piano riffs started and my tears began to fall, the video so simply beautiful. The video ended and I looked across the screen where I saw in the suggestions Demi Lovato's *Believe In Me*. I clicked the song, not expecting it to be everything I needed, but the lyrics explained everything I was feeling: 'I don't wanna be afraid, I wanna wake up feeling beautiful today and know that I'm okay, 'cause everyone's perfect in unusual ways. You see I just wanna believe in me'.

Once the song ended I found myself looking across once again for inspiration and wasn't disappointed; another suggestion of Demi Lovato's *Warrior* came up at the side. I clicked it, hoping it would continue my need for strength, those lyrics reaching me unlike anything had before: 'Now I'm a warrior. Now I've got thicker skin, I'm a warrior, I'm stronger than I've ever been, and my armour is made of steel, you can't get in, I'm a warrior and you can never hurt me again'. At this point I was a mess, in that I was overwhelmed with the raw relatable lyrics I had listened to. I'd looked across the screen one last time, what caught my eye shocked me, 'Demi Lovato opens up about self-harm'. I reluctantly clicked the video - shaking, crying - I listened as Demi described what I had been doing, how it had felt; I was floored. This woman, who I'd only known as a Disney princess, had just, in a few songs and an interview, explained what I had wanted to say for years. I had no idea of all the things Demi had suffered with over the years, but her honesty gave me hope to continue.

That moment changed my life forever. I started to work on myself from that point, becoming more and more infatuated with Demi's message of positivity and hope. Learning, with every song, that I too could be a warrior. I was doing well, my self-harm became controllable, my brain wasn't in a constant state of failure; that is, until one day in May, that day I couldn't control the urge anymore. I'd lost it with myself; frustrated and confused I had hurt myself again.

A few months passed and I was 100 days clean. I celebrated with getting 'Now I'm A Warrior' tattooed across my heart. At this time I was talking to a friend who lived in America. We'd met on Twitter, as she was a Lovatic (Demi's fan base) too. I had arranged to go and visit and, in the September, that finally came true. Little did I know that her mum had paid for me to go to Demi's concert in NC that week. But, not only that, also to go to a meet and greet too! I was absolutely shocked that someone could do something so incredible for me.

The day came, September 12th, we'd spent all night working on posters and singing along to songs we knew we were going to hear live in just a few hours' time. We lined up for the meet and greet. Behind a curtain we could hear this voice we'd heard so many times before. It was my turn, I stepped into the small room:

Demi: *Hi!*

Me: *Hel~*

D: *Awww you have the same tattoo as me!* (Pointing at 'Now I'm a Warrior')

M: *Yeah, and I have the lovatic heart on my wrist!*

D: *That's so cool*

Me: *Yeah, I got them for being over 100 days clean....*

D: *That's amazing! Well done!*

M: *Thank you so much*

D: *You don't sound like you're from North Carolina...*

M: *No, I'm English*

D: *Oh my god, that's so cool! Thank you!* (Hugs me tight)

Then we take the picture and I reluctantly leave... The concert of course was incredible! I went back home with the biggest of hearts and the memory that Demi was proud.

October 17th 2014, the day that everything came crashing down again, I had been struggling to fight the urge after some arguments and problems at work and I felt worse than ever. I couldn't fight the thoughts anymore and that night once more they won. They may have won this battle, but they were not winning the war. A few days after I was feeling so mad at myself, thinking I'd thrown away all those days before, that Demi and others would be so disappointed in me; but then something clicked, I wasn't going to let this win again! I decided to challenge myself to beat my previous record, and I did.

That was the last time I ever self-harmed.

In January 2015, I decided that I wanted to speak up; after thinking about it for so long I pushed myself to make my very first video. It gained thousands of views overnight with people from school watching it, apologising and commenting nothing but love. I decided to keep posting videos onto a motivational Facebook page I had created called *Abbie Foster's StayStrong*, as well as reaching out to charities and different media to share my story of hope and recovery. I was finally feeling good, minimal depression, no suicidal thoughts and a brand new joy for life, knowing I could do anything.

I started working with an incredible charity called Fixers who have really supported me along the way; they've given me so much confidence. Since then, over the years, I have worked with many different organisations sharing my story and using it to inspire others. Most recently I have been working with the Norfolk And Suffolk NHS Foundation Trust, helping to improve the service as well as being part of their Youth Council, and I work with the BBC in different projects including radio and TV appearances. Today I love my life. I have the most incredible fiancé, friends and family support around me; they support my dreams and every crazy idea I may have. I have a great outlook on my future and I can't wait to see what I do next. Recovery and positivity are incredible things; once you open your mind to the possibility of a great life amazing things can happen!

You got this. Staystrong, always.

Abbie x

*Keep up to date with what Abbie is doing here: https://www.facebook.com/AbbieFostersStayStrong/*

# Bev is Kinda Proud of her journey from burnout to a burning desire to help others know that it's 'okay to not be okay'

*After spending years as a 'successful' business woman, hardly ever allowing herself to take time off, it took all of Bev's strength from deep within to reach out for help at a time when she felt all was lost. Bev discovered that this was true strength. Like so many who have #Emerged Proud through a personal crisis, this has now become Bev's mission; to help others to realise that mental health struggles are a normal reaction to difficult life*

*circumstances, and that it's not only okay to self-care, it's absolutely vital.*

*Bev now tells her story within workplace settings, to give others strength to reach out. Here she recounts how she ended up doing this wonderful work...*

Like a Phoenix from the ashes

This year (2019) marks a huge milestone for me as it was ten years ago that I went through what can only be described as my annus horribilis.

2009, the year that changed my life in so many ways; I started the year, what I thought was happy enough, although looking back the toxic relationship I was in, along with the high-pressured job and bullying I was enduring in the workplace, was not conducive to a happy, balanced life.

As the start of the year passed, I went through it convincing myself it would all be okay, that things would work out alright in the end if I just hung in there, and hung in there I did. I hung on for the first five months of the year by a thread; it was like I was on the edge of a rock face gripping on by my fingertips. At the end of May 2009, my life fell apart when the situation at work became unbearable, so much so that all I did was spend all my time in tears, sobbing my way through the day and into my pillow at night.

Finally, I gave in and visited the doctor, who diagnosed clinical depression and severe anxiety. I found this to be just the start of a road that led to a journey of darkness that went seemingly deeper with each day. I found myself walking through a fog; a fog of what I believed to be failure, a fog of sadness, a fog of paranoia, a fog of loneliness and a fog of isolation that turned into a fog of anger.

I became so angry. I was angry with me for being so useless, I was angry with those in work who had seemingly turned against me. I was angry with those closest to me who, in my mind, didn't understand. I was angry with God, the Universe and basically anyone else I could blame for the situation I was now in.

Following my diagnosis, I was informed by the doctor that I had two weeks before hospitalisation, so my choice was to take a sick note and sign off from work, or to go to work where, within two weeks, they would be sending an ambulance to pick me up! I knew in my heart the choice was no choice, but it was hard, I always resisted the urge to be off sick but no more, I had to give in.

During the latter part of 2009 I lost my job, my home (temporarily to dry rot), and my relationship; my income lowered dramatically as I went from a senior manager salary to employment support allowance, and in my mind my world fell apart. Little did I know this was actually the time when the foundations of my new life were starting to form.

I found myself self-harming, literally dragging my nails against my skin until I drew blood. This was my way of proving to myself I could hurt myself more than anyone else could hurt me. In the darkest of nights, I found suicide thoughts creeping into my mind. I had it all planned, I wrote the text I would send to family and friends, then worked out exactly how I would do it. I was so close and yet the thought of the sadness I would cause to others somehow kept me hanging on to life.

Christmas/New Year 2010 became a turning point in my life. As I celebrated with family and friends I vowed that I would do whatever it would take to ensure that I would never have another year like 2009. I would turn my life around and ensure that those that had helped drive me down that road would not win. They may well have won the battle that took me towards the darkness of life, but they were never going to win the war.

I started 2010 by signing up to a Life Coaching diploma course as I became determined to help others not go where I had been. I wanted to somehow let others know it is okay not to be okay, and you can indeed start, day by day, to come out the other side. At the time, I renovated my property by day, so it became habitable again, and studied for my diploma by night. I was on medication for the depression and I have to say I was very lucky to have such an understanding doctor who was always on hand when needed. I undertook counselling sessions, through which I learnt to take baby steps along the road to recovery.

I was shown how to take each day at a time, how to take steps towards a new goal every day, even if that goal was just taking a walk in the park rather than staying under my duvet. One of my counsellors suggested always writing in my diary a plan for the next day the evening before, therefore giving me a reason to get up. I have to say this advice worked so well in that I started to find getting up in the morning was fun as I suddenly had a purpose; it meant at the end of the day I could reflect on my progress and give thanks for all I had achieved that day.

As time passed, in 2010 I spent more and more quality time with family and friends. This made me realise that those riches in life lie with people, not materialistic objects of desire. These lovely people, along with those I had met in my dark times, started to build on the foundations I was building within myself. I read books and absorbed information around positive thinking, faith, belief and mindfulness. I learnt how self-care was something that had been missing from my life for a long time and how reintroducing it would support me during the next stage of my journey, as I began to walk along the path of recovery.

Fast forward to 2019 and, suffice to say, that the last ten years have been a rollercoaster, during which there were times I had to find the strength to hold on a little tighter. I have endured heartache, debt, and the anxiety still lurks hidden in the shadows, but today it is thankfully manageable.

I started a business in August 2010 through which I now indeed do help others in many ways, including workplace wellbeing. I am proud to say that I actively share my story to normalise the importance of good mental health and what happens if self-care isn't treated as an important part of everyday life.

I became a published author in 2012, an award-winning mentor, a radio show host, an avid volunteer, and met many new friends along the way. I renovated and sold my apartment to move back to my childhood village, where I now live near my parents and share my life with my wonderful partner and his children. I know I am blessed and I offer gratitude every day for the life I now have, the life I have built from the ashes; indeed the life that, through experience, turned an ordinary life to an *extraordinary* one.

I know from experience what it is like to feel like all is lost and I have seen members of my family broken by the suicide of my young cousin. The grief it leaves for others is immeasurable and I am so relieved that, from deep within, I found a strength that saw me reach out for help at the time when I felt all was lost.

If I hadn't done that I'd have missed out on all that the last ten years has brought me, and for that again I give thanks.

*To contact Bev, you can find her website here:  http://www.awakencoaching.co.uk*

*or Email: bev@awakencoaching.co.uk*

*Linkedin www.linkedin.com/in/beverley-jones/*

## Louis is Kinda Proud that his troubled past has made him who he is today

*Multiple brushes with death led Louis to his purpose and helped him to find meaning in life. Once full of guilt and exhausted with searching for who he was, but finally learning to love and accept himself as he is, means that Louis now lives a life happier than he could have imagined. He's found his purpose in creating music and art to spread messages of LOVE and HOPE to others who are struggling like he once was...*

Growing up was never going to be an easy win

for me. From the age of four I was dressing up in my big sister's clothes, and shuffling around in my mum's high heels. Most days a Barbie doll would accompany me to school, and this would invite a lot of ridicule. Reaching my high school years, I had already endured a constant eight years of bullying. Never feeling good enough, or strong enough to speak out, I kept this to myself for many years until I told my parents about the nightmare my school life was.

I had always had a passion for singing and acting, so at the age of ten I enrolled into a local theatre school and quickly built up my confidence to take on lead roles. This newly-found confidence would slowly and surely crumble as I began high school at the age of eleven. Through a series of traumatic events whilst abroad, my parents broke up and filed for divorce. This happening within the first two months of starting high school really affected my overall years in education. I became very secluded, depressed, and alcoholic. I remember days where I would arrive at school and be sent right back home by a teacher because I stank of booze and was clearly inebriated. I was also an extremely rebellious and secretive teenager, so all of this went on for years before my mother and sisters knew.

Reaching almost sixteen, I was at my all time low. I had been self-harming and drinking excessively for many years now, and had also been seeing a psychiatric doctor. In the winter of 2011, months before my sixteenth birthday, I was groomed and sexually assaulted by a man three times my age. At the time, I brushed this off and almost acted like it had never even happened. I continued doing this for another eight years until finally opening up about it and taking action. I believe this was a huge trigger for me that resulted in me taking my first overdose in April 2012. The last thing I remember is slashing my arm open so wide that blood was pouring and squirting out all over my mum's living room. The next thing, I was in hospital throwing up my guts and itching like crazy all over my body. I had washed down a huge concoction of paracetamol, ibuprofen, tramadol, diazepam, amongst other things, with a litre bottle of whiskey. The tramadol had caused me to itch so much that I scratched my head and face until it bled.

I hated the way I was treated by some of the staff in hospital. I was looked down on because I wasn't valuing my life at such a young age. I was also on a ward surrounded by elderly men dying of terrible causes. So I already felt the guilt of being the one person there not grateful for life and actually trying to die! One man from the crisis team actually took me into a private room and lectured me about how selfish I was and how I was ruining my family's lives.

Because of the poor care plan that was put in place after my discharge from hospital, I just sank lower and lower. Within the next four years I went on to attempt suicide another six times. I also left dreaded high school, went on to study music at college, but then started training as a hairdresser! I call this my gap year because it was between graduating college and going to university when I didn't know what to do with my life. When I finally made it to London at the age of nineteen, I felt like my life would turn around. I'd always dreamed of moving to London and it was finally a reality. However, the freedom of being a student, and the social life that goes with it, took its toll on me. I began drinking excessively again and would often become very depressed. I lasted two years studying in London until my soul felt like it was exhausted and I needed to leave the city behind. This was also the time around my twenty first birthday, when I travelled to New Orleans for the first time and met my fiancé, Price. Falling in love with him, and his city, was definitely a contributor in dropping out of university. However, I had been considering this before I met him and was already looking for a change of scenery.

Strangely enough, none of my near-death experiences (NDEs) were special, or transcendent. It was the aftermath that shaped me, and the recovery was when I heard my calling and received my message. For a long time after my first NDE, a beautiful Victorian lady dressed in pink would appear on my stairs landing every night. I've often wondered if it was a past family member because she felt so familiar. I named this lady Maria, and she was the first one to protect me after my first suicide attempt. I regularly had, what I believe to be, demonic entities surrounding me, feeding off of my low, negative state. I truly believe when we are not in good places in our lives, it can be an invitation for dark spirits to latch on to you. The insidious haunting I experienced during my dark times my mum and I named 'Jimmy'. He eventually departed and left me alone, but it was the petrifying tribulations and challenges he put me through that made me the strong and defiant person I am today.

I am still very much connected to spirit and see these abilities grow all the time. It is my ultimate belief that my series of NDEs sent me on a journey of self discovery. It was never going to happen overnight, but over the last eight years I have honed my skills, figured out who I am and where I want to be, and dedicated myself to that. In order to spread my message and help change the world, I needed to love and accept myself, and push my mission forward every step of the way until I get to the platform I need to reach huge audiences. In my life I want to create music for people to relate to, I want to make art that makes people feel things, I want to act in movies that make a difference and highlight important issues, I want to be an activist and fight for human rights; and as a gay man I feel very strongly about this. I believe we are all equal, and all deserve the same treatment in life. I have become empowered and I am still transcending; I want to take over the world with love and light.

I am grateful for my troubling past because it has made me happier than I could ever imagine and taken me to places I have only dreamed of. I count my blessings every day and continue to work on myself to become the best version of myself possible.

I want to help others do the same. If everyone could accept themselves and hear this message, we could collectively change the world and make it a more peaceful utopia for the future generations.

## Louis' bio:

I am a 23 year old Jazz singer, wig stylist, poet, & artist located in Lincoln, U.K., and New Orleans, U.S.A. My destructive, and almost 'demonic', adolescence gave me the tools I needed to survive in this world, and spread a message of peace and love through music, art, and expression. What I experienced in my teens drastically shifted my entire perception and beliefs about life, and its purpose.

# Samaya's depression was the 'medicine' that was pushing her to be true to herself

*Like Samaya, so many of us get nudges from our 'Soul voice', pushing us to live a life more authentically aligned with who we truly are. Doing so can cause chaos and pain as we choose to move away from 'fitting in' with the social dictations we've often been brought up with. It's learning to recognise that the pain of these messages can be the thing that liberates us, if we really listen, as Samaya recounts through her personal journey here...*

# THE VISIT

It was spring of 1993 when I got my first visit.

I was fifteen and having a tumultuous time trying to make sense of it all, when an inquisitive voice from deep within surfaced and started pulling me and my life into pieces.

It was my soul's voice, which was asking me to start making meaning of what was worth valuing and loving, so I could start building my life with those things at the very heart of it all.

This was a task that I had not been prepared for and had no idea how to even start tackling. At that time, I hadn't known anyone who had gone through anything quite like this.

What did I love? I had no clue.

But the voice was there and it was insisting. It was not barging. It was not lessening. It was like an uninvited guest who did not seem to be aware that they were gate-crashing. If anything, it seemed to feel right at home.

This persistent enquiry, that came almost out of the blue, pushed me into an intense process of searching and deconstruction that ended up leaving me exhausted, depressed and quite vulnerable. What was worse, I was not coming up with the goods, and that was slowly killing me on the inside. At fifteen

I felt like I had no clue about the things that really mattered, what I loved, what was worthy of love, and the true value in my life. Not just anyone's life, but mine.

Most people I knew seemed to live life according to a book written by society and not their own soul. Where was I going to get help from? This deep search was not yielding successful results and it started affecting my external life so much so that, at 15, I seriously contemplated taking my own life and got really close to overdosing myself to death. I was only to be saved, last minute, by a phone call from a friend who had previously also tried taking her own life.

I did not mention on that call what I was about to do and my friend, who had slowly moved away from our friendship after her own attempt, admitted she did not know why she had rung me, she just knew that she had to do so. I definitely look back on that call as an angelic intervention.

On the same day of the call, my soul came back with yet another message. This time, however, it did not bring a question, but a piece of advice. I was told that this did not need to sit as a heavy load on my shoulders. That I had a lot of my life ahead of me and that the answers did not need rushing, I just needed to give myself permission to take my time. This made a lot of sense to me and I somehow tried to go on living my life.

Fast forward fifteen years, I found myself living in a new country that felt like my spiritual home, living as a practising Buddhist. Until then, soul would communicate to me in many indirect ways through music, art, books, poetry and other people; through their eyes, their movements, their words. But very rarely did I get to channel direct messages from it just like that time when I was fifteen and scared to face myself and the big world.

One day, following the end of an intense work stint in the psychiatric wards of a London hospital, I got another visit. My soul was there to touch base with me again, picking up from where we had left off and bringing up the question that it was no stranger to me. 'What in my life was worth living for?'

I was now of course 15 years older, yet despite the many more experiences I had under my belt, the depth of that enquiry yet again brought up a ton of fear. Perhaps because this time around the question had lead me to another more relevant enquiry. This new enquiry had to do with what value I was actually giving to the world, rather than what was being given to me, which is how I had seen it the first time around.

But I had yet to fully make my life my own and to tap into the potential that was lying within me, underneath it all. I realised that I had not learned how to serve my own soul by showing up in the world in a way that fulfilled me. The meditation I had been practising for years had helped me tap into myself, yet was now gradually getting me to want to create a more personable life, full of meaning, depth and purpose. A life of creativity that stemmed from a deep connection with my soul, in a way that brought me and others joy. I was being urged to create a much more personable life that lived on a daily communion with my soul and purpose. Where I wouldn't have to be tested like this over and over again.

This realisation and desire to align with my soul's creativity and start living my life as a work of art, had become really clear. I had come here in the world to create after all. But first I had to take a little detour again. I was triggered into yet another depression, which lasted for 2 years. I had to stop work and immerse myself into my healing; face my demons, get to know my fears and sabotages so I could understand myself better and go the distance.

I realised that I held the belief that I did not have much to offer the world. That I couldn't create and build good things. And I feared that I was going to move through life without fulfilling my deeper purpose. During that time, I was hanging on for dear life and often the intensity of the situation got me exhausted trying to stay afloat. During an intensive silent meditation retreat with an esteemed teacher, I asked to be given permission to return home early because I found myself starting to plot throwing myself in the Scottish lochs and drowning in the river.

Upon my return, what hit home with me was that if I was going to put all this energy to try and get the strength I needed to take my own life, I might as well put that energy into healing and keeping myself alive. This realisation ended up becoming the actual fuel that helped me make my life turn around. I then started discovering many more gifts which soon made it apparent that my depression had turned into my actual medicine. Shamans and Medicine men and women around the world say that when we lose our way, for a human to be truly born and married into their spirit and true self and find our true path, we often have to reach a state of emergency, where we are forced and initiated to activate our true spirit self. It's like the urgency, brought to us through an illness, a loss, an intense life experience, forces us to truly become ourselves.

Since these two visits, I am pleased to say I have been on a very different life trajectory. There is a noticeable change and grounded-ness in my own soul and path, despite the various challenges that have presented my way. It has not meant that life has become easier, but my capacity to process things is more robust, whilst I seem to maintain a more continuous and deeper communion with my soul, as well as my spirit path.

I have a lot more fun creating, which doesn't seem so scary anymore.

And as far as my soul conversations go, these days they are more fun and enjoyable, reminding me daily we are here to play and fulfil our destiny by leaving our energy signature and blueprint in the world and shining our light bright.

Would my light shine as bright had it not been for the darkness I had encountered? I will leave this for you to decide. I have learned that my darkness is not to be feared, as it holds the most healing medicine, able to transform me over and over again to my deepest, truest self.

Thank you for reading my story. I hope it guides you through your own tough times and inspires you to choose to be returning back to your light, time and time again.

Love

Samaya Adelin

*Find out more about Samaya and contact her here: www.samayaadelin.com*

# Colin's journey through darkness helped him find his brightest light

*Finding the strength to talk about his struggles and go on to tell his story has enabled Colin not only to help himself, but set him on his mission to help others, through the creation of his very own App: DEpressON*

*Here's Colin's story in his own words...*

It was the 21st of June 2016, around 12pm, I had been struggling with depression and anxiety badly for the last few months, and had begun to lose hope, each day was getting harder and harder, I was losing control, and everything seemed like it was falling apart around me. Then, one day on my lunch break at work I had to cross a motorway bridge to get my lunch: halfway across that bridge I stopped, and decided to end all of the pain.

As I stood and looked down on the motorway below me, I started to watch all of the cars passing under the bridge I was stood on. For some reason, as I was crossing the motorway bridge, I'd suddenly stopped, just over halfway to look over. I'd now been stood there for a good few minutes, and as I watched the traffic go by, I'd started to think of the people in those cars; I'd started to think about how their lives probably had meaning, they were happy and they were enjoying their lives, they were going somewhere today and were looking forward to getting to their destination, wherever that was.

I started to think about my life, or what had become of it at least. I tried to think about: Where was I going? Where was my destination? Where had my happiness gone? Why did I no longer feel like I had a purpose? I thought about my family and friends trying to convince me I did have a reason to live, but that suddenly turned into the thought of how much I'd let them down, how much of a failure I was. They had offered support when I'd first been diagnosed with my depression, and even though I'd chosen to fight this battle on my own, I remembered the words I used to tell my wife, that I'd be ok when she offered her support: 'It's in my head and I am the strongest person I know. I will sort it out'.

I thought I'd coped quite well but the last few weeks I'd felt myself falling, and I didn't want to tell people I needed help, that would just make me look weak. I continued to watch the traffic as people walked past me on the bridge. My head at this point felt like it couldn't cope with processing all the thoughts that were overloading it, and I remember looking up to the sky which was cloudy that day, but you could still see the sun shining through. As I looked up, I just wanted my head to clear, I wanted to stop my hands from shaking, I wanted to not feel like a failure, but most of all I wanted to protect my family from being affected by all the pain I was feeling.

As I drew my eyes back to the motorway I noticed my shaking hands were no longer shaking but instead had taken a tight grip of the railing on the bridge, my left foot was now placed on the bottom of the railing and, suddenly, maybe I had found a solution, I could make all the noise from my head go away, I could protect my family from my pain by simply taking the problem away. I felt myself leaning towards the motorway. Maybe I'd just found my destination.

Since that day, things in my life have totally changed. Since I found the strength to speak out and admit that I needed help; that, alone, I was struggling to deal with these feelings. I walked from that bridge straight into my office at work and picked up the phone. I was lucky that I had medical insurance through work. I'd been given the leaflets and numbers to call many weeks ago, but had chosen not to use them, but now in that office I'd decided I had to make use of whatever help was available to me. After a conversation with the very nice lady on the other end of the phone I was referred to a shrink. At first I was against the idea, as in my mind seeing a shrink was all about being crazy and would involve me lying on a couch identifying ink blots but, despite this, I knew I needed to try anything in the form of help. I needed to accept the advice given to me.

On my first visit with the shrink, after I'd spoken about my feelings and my childhood etc., I remember a look on his face as he looked down on his notes from the session, then looked up at me; the look said it all, he was looking at me as if to say: 'How have you made it to 42 without seeking help before?!!!!!' At the end of the session I was diagnosed with clinical depression and acute anxiety; I'd been promoted! He recommended I attend group therapy, and I will always remember what he said to me that day about this form of therapy: 'You will meet some great new friends and will really enjoy these sessions'. I remember thinking: 'How's that going to work - you're going to stick 10 or 12 miserable people in a room and expect them to make friends with each other?!!!!!' I imagined how the phone calls to each other would go: 'Hi, what're you up to today?' 'I'm avoiding bridges, what about you?' I really didn't believe these sessions would help, or that I'd make any kind of new friends, but I had to try them.

Unbeknownst to me, those group sessions were about to change my life in so many ways. Meeting that group of people on that first day I would never have imagined how it would help turn my journey with depression and anxiety into such an amazing adventure. Those sessions were really the beginning of something amazing. Whilst in the sessions I soon realised that, although the therapist leading the sessions was needed, it was in fact the group that began to really support each other: we found strength and support in each other, we found using humour about our situations helped, because we were all on this journey together. We found an openness when talking about ourselves; an openness to be honest I don't really think I'd had for a very long time. That room quickly became where we could be ourselves, without fear of judgment or ridicule. Once we entered that room we left the stigma attached to these 'conditions' behind, and without that weight on our shoulders, and with each others' support, we began to find it easier to move forward.

It was that support and how we began to work together that gave me the idea of DEpressON, an app that would embrace our experiences and learnings. We had been advised to download several different forms of apps that could possibly help us, but both myself and others in the group found these apps clinical and sterile in their approach and look. We tried them but each one felt too detached from our real needs: they lacked something and we all quickly stopped using them. I suggested in one of the groups my idea for DEpressON and was taken aback, if I'm being honest, by the enthusiasm and excitement towards the idea, not just by the group but also by the professionals leading the sessions. The last few sessions of our CBT almost turned into a workshop around the app, with everyone adding ideas and suggestions, and the idea began to grow from there.

This is where my journey really became an adventure. Who would have thought that day on the bridge would end up with me having my own business, being invited all around the country to talk publicly about this Journey? I wouldn't, but the darkness actually helped me find the brightest light. My story, because I found the strength to tell it, has not only changed my life but many others so far, and I know it will change many more. At the beginning of this journey my wife and I were getting divorced. We are now still happily married, and now have a new addition to our family, Poppy. Her middle name is for a reason; it's Hope. Because together we make a difference, together we make this journey an adventure.

**If we have hope, we have tomorrow, let's make tomorrow Amazing.**

Colin's bio:

My own experience with depression, and its potentially life-ending consequences, took me on a journey that I now call my journey to self-discovery.

The importance of support is essential to healing and that's my plan. It's all I have been concentrating on for the last year; talking, meeting and connecting with people and industry experts. I want to help people with DEpressOn – PRESSon. Let's walk together and make a difference.

*To find out more about Colin's work go to: www.depresson.co.uk*

*Email: info@depresson.co.uk*

*Twitter: @DEpressON2*

# David is KindaProud that he came through a life of hopelessness to celebrate the miracle that he truly is

*David from Manchester, UK, is a shining example of having #Emerged Proud through a life of adversity to use his journey to do good things in the world; from numerous suicide attempts due to feeling a sense of hopelessness and helplessness, he's gone on to be the head of services for a thriving residential support unit. What a transformation journey! David's story goes to show that, whatever your circumstances, there is always hope of a better life...*

I used to consider myself the ultimate contradiction. I loved life and I hated life. In the early years I tried many ways to avoid day-to-day life. I found sanctuary at home with my family, but oftentimes this was the place that represented danger.

I found distraction through friendships and thrill-seeking behaviour, which led to life in gangs, drugs and crime. I felt safe and accepted and part of something bigger and greater than myself in the gang life that I became part of. This lifestyle soon became one of those things that I also loved and hated most, and presented even more danger than anything I had ever experienced.

Between the ages of 12 to 15 I went through various phases of trying different substances, ranging from cannabis, LSD, glue and alcohol. When I was 15 I was introduced to Heroin. When I was 17 I was introduced to Crack cocaine. There are many ways to describe the effects of Heroin and Crack and everyone who has experienced them will have their own way that is personal to them. For me, it felt like the ultimate high and low; the best and the worst all rolled into one. This started the longest phase of drug use I was ever to experience.

Once again my life became a contradiction. I loved and hated Heroin and Crack. I loved and hated the things I did to fund my drug use. I loved and hated the lifestyle, the ups and downs, the twists and turns, the certainty and the uncertainty, the fun and the fear. My life was a paradox.

When I was 22 I hit my first rock bottom. I became so desperate, so full of guilt, shame and remorse that I just wanted to die. I took an overdose. I woke up in a police cell. I didn't know how I got there. When I came round the police told me I had driven my car whilst under the influence of the drugs I'd taken to overdose and I drove head on into a brick wall. I was eventually released without charge and without any follow-up or referral to drug/alcohol or mental health services.

I continued along the same path until I was 26, when I hit another rock bottom. My drug use and lifestyle had spiralled even further out of control. It was the worst it had ever been. I was on bail for theft offences when I was arrested again for breaching my bail by committing further offences. When the policeman searched me on admission to the police station, he missed the cord in my tracksuit bottoms. After being in the cell for a while I started to withdraw from the Heroin. Once again I started to experience the feelings of hopelessness. This, coupled with the 'cold turkey', sent me over the edge. I looked around the cell for a ligature point and noticed the sink. I took the cord from my tracksuit pants and tied it around one of the taps and then tied it around my neck and sat down. The next thing I remember was coming round on the floor in the cell with paramedics resuscitating me and then being rushed to hospital. After a period in A&E I was taken back to the Police station and kept in custody overnight. In court the next morning I was sentenced to a community order and released. There was no follow-up, or referral to drug/alcohol or mental health services.

I continued along the same path until I was 35. For long periods during my addiction I made the choice to stay on the streets, or in run-down Crack houses in Moss Side for days/weeks/months on end because it felt easier than going home and facing my family. It was the year 2000 and, once again, I had been on bail for theft offences and, yet again, I had breached bail. I was placed on remand in Strangeways. I had been in for about 4 days and was still withdrawing. My cellmate had gone to court on the Friday and was released, which meant I was on my own in the cell for the weekend. Over the years I have spent many days/nights/weeks/months/years in prison.

Suicidal ideation was never about being in custody. For me, it is more about the hopelessness and helplessness that I feel when that veil descends. I still experience that to this day. On this occasion I was at an all-time low. The two most important people in my life: my mum and my nana had both passed away in 1992 and I had spent the last 8 years in grief, drifting further and further into the darkest and loneliest times of my life. People had stopped coming to visit me when I was in prison during those days. My last remaining family had just about taken all they could handle of me. I was overcome by waves of despair and, in that moment, I decided once again that I'd had enough. It was the early hours of the morning, 'the nightshift' for an addict in cold turkey. I took a razor blade apart and I cut my sheets up and made them into a ligature. The sheets were made of fire retardant material and they were really strong. I tied one end around the bars in the window and the other end around my neck as high up as I could manage. There was nothing to stand on in the cell as all the furniture was made of steel and was fixed securely to the walls. I pulled the ligature as tight as I could and then I sat down as best and as low as I could manage. I started to drift off into the comforting nothingness of black out and then suddenly found myself in a heap on the floor. The sheet had snapped. I was absolutely beside myself. For the life of me I couldn't work out how the sheet snapped? I was thrown into confusion and then the deepest feelings of despair and hopelessness that I had ever experienced. I felt like such a failure and I cried and cried for what seemed like forever.

The next thing I remember was an overwhelming feeling of calmness and peace, like I have never ever felt before or since. I was then overcome by a strange and inexplicable sense that everything was going to be OK. To this day I don't know where that came from. Whether it was my faith, an angel, or from God himself, but it was so strong and reassuring that I just started to feel better, like I was in good hands and I was being looked after.

I eventually got up off the floor and tidied things up, brushed myself off and sat down at the steel table to roll a cigarette. I noticed the local paper, The Manchester Evening News, in front of me on the table. I hadn't noticed this paper at any point before now. I started reading through it and, around a third of the way through, I came across a story by a woman who had opened a day centre in Stockport for recovering addicts and alcoholics. The woman in the story was also in recovery from addiction. There and then I wrote her a letter asking for help. Two weeks later she came to see me. When I walked into the visit room and saw her for the first time she had an aura like I have never ever seen before. When I talked to her about the behaviours, thoughts and feelings and the lifestyle that came with my addiction, it was like she already knew me and she had already lived most of my story herself.

Four weeks later, I was escorted from Strangeways to Manchester Crown Court for sentence. I was supported in court by a representative from the day centre and there were reports from my drug workers in the prison and the community and my probation officer all supporting placement at the day centre. For the first time ever in my life I was placed before a Judge who spoke to me in a way that I have never been spoken to by a Judge, and I had been before enough of them in my time! This man seemed to really pay attention to the situation, rather than just to the problem. He gave me a chance and sentenced me to a community order so that I could attend the day centre.

I attended the rehab the next day for the first time and then daily for the next six months. I went on to attend aftercare two days a week for a further three months. After completing nine months in treatment I was offered the opportunity to volunteer with the service, which I accepted. Twelve months later I was offered a full time paid role as a support worker with their very first supported housing project. Six months later I was offered the role of deputy manager. Twelve months later I was offered the role of manager. Three years later I was promoted to head of service, responsible for managing 72 beds across Greater Manchester.

I left the service in 2011 to pursue other opportunities and I have managed several projects and services since. I now manage a 16 bed residential rehab as a CQC registered manager for one of the biggest health and social care providers in the country. Our service was inspected by CQC in May 2019 and we were graded as good across all 5 domains. Our rehab is one of the longest standing residential rehabs in the history of residential services to still be operating in the UK.

Away from my life as a professional, I have since remarried. My wife and I have 7 children and 8 grandchildren between us. I have undertaken lots of personal development work and I have completed various rites of passage and initiation ceremonies in the 19 years that I have been in recovery. I am an active member and co-facilitator of abandofbrothers and I have the shared responsibility for the growth and development of abandofbrothers in Manchester. I still experience fleeting feelings of hopelessness and helplessness and not wanting to be alive today. I have learned to live with and to embrace my shadow, but more importantly I have learned to love that part of me. Thoughts of suicide are a constant companion. For me the blessing is that I have not tried to take my life since that dark and desperate night when I was last in prison in 2000. Today I am grateful for everything that life throws at me and I have learned to celebrate myself as the miracle that I am.

David now:

I currently manage a CQC registered 16 bed residential rehab in Oldham Greater Manchester by the name of Leigh Bank, which is a Turning Point service. Responsibilities include managing the rehab team, day-to-day operational functions, alongside all of the internal governance and quality assurance. I have experience of preparing for, and overseeing, CQC inspections and, to date, all CQC reports have resulted in good standards of service across all 5 domains.

My approach to life is based on connection with people and with communities. I take the approach that our communities are rich in resources and that we should be the co-producers of our own health and wellbeing, rather than the recipients of services. I promote connection through community networks, relationships and friendships which empowers people and provides caring mutual help.

*Find out more about David and his Band of Brothers at:*

*http://abandofbrothers.org.uk/*

*Facebook: https://www.facebook.com/ABOBcommunity*

*Twitter @band_brothersuk*

*www.turning-point.co.uk*

*www.cqc.org.uk/location/1-3955478171http://
wellbeing.turning-point.co.uk/residential*

**Kelly is KindaProud that she's learned to glean the gifts from her pain, and urges you to trust in the wisdom of nature's grand design**

*Kelly's story will undoubtedly resonate with many of you; trying for years to push away what are so readily perceived as 'wrong', 'bad' or 'negative' emotions, led Kelly further and further down a path of despair. It was only when Kelly realised that there were gifts in her emotions; messages nudging her back onto her Soul path, that she learned to embrace them and in turn love herself. As Kelly so rightly says:*

134

*'We can never know where this life will take us unless we choose to continue on'*…

Journeying through pain was not something that I had anticipated would be such a big part of my life. Like many people, my life has been filled with challenges, from being painfully shy and self-conscious as a child to experiencing a lot of loss from deaths in my immediate family.

I guess I just thought I could simply find an escape route, something that would take the pain away.

My first way of dealing with this pain was avoidance. I did this through overeating, drinking large amounts of alcohol, and looking for escape in the arms of men. This was how I lived for 30 years or more.

Distraction came in many forms, and even came through the spiritual journey by me hopping on the 'positivity bandwagon', thinking I could 'bright-light' the darkness away with affirmations and visualisations.

I think the day it hit me that all these distractions were no longer working was the first of many times that I considered suicide. I remember lying in my bed wondering why I should continue living; I could not see a reason why.

In my mind, I simply believed I was a complete failure. Nothing worked for me and I was not fitting in with the 'norm' of what I perceived I should be doing in my life at the time. Sitting in bed one day I hit my head with any object I could find near me, to knock the pain away. This felt like the only option. I never contemplated suicide deeply, but it remained an escape that I often considered.

Depression, anxiety and the failure story that I had believed for so long, really wore me down, until I started practising mindfulness. I began to see a pattern in my thoughts, repeating over and over again. I could see that those thoughts were an illusion, not real, but I still couldn't fully embrace what was happening with the compassion that I knew, deep-down, I really needed.

That was until I lay in my bed during a lengthy dark period of depression and through tears and crying into my pillow I screamed out loud, 'Why is this happening? What is the gift here?' And, what I discovered was that the answer came in the form of space. It was like a pause that took place inside of me; that the space between the pain and the next thought gave me an opening which showed me that this feeling, this pain, was not all there was.

I had found the right question. Before, my question had been, 'What is wrong with me?' but 'What is the gift here?' – that question stopped me in my tracks...

As humans we are encouraged to rush through life, making happiness our goal, or receiving momentary pleasures. We are shown that to 'be happy' we need certain things; stuff, people, material objects, to live a worthwhile life, but it's not true.

These momentary pleasures are simply filling the void that needs entering from within. The gap, the journey, the time when we are genuinely and wholeheartedly giving ourselves space to simply be with whatever arises, regardless of how painful it is, is the key.

One major recognition came for me when I realised that the thoughts of wanting to escape from the pain were the very things causing the struggle, but that there was no struggle when I stopped and allowed the pain, the pain that needed to be felt, to be witnessed, to be held, to be owned.

We are far too keen to grab onto happiness or joy or peace, and we desperately want to rid ourselves of pain, fear, anger, rage and sadness, but life, in its wisdom, knows that our attachments to these emotions is perpetuating the suffering we feel.

I used to hate who I was. I envied those who seemed to love themselves, have self-confidence and felt happy with their lives. I yearned so much to love who I was and to feel enough, but in my attempt to escape the darkness, I missed the very road into the jewels that lie within the pain.

Like diamonds that are born in the darkness of the earth, it is often the sorrow, the anger, the fear, that brings us our greatest challenge, but also our greatest learning. Once I started to view each feeling as a long-lost child in an orphanage of rejected emotions, I began to have compassion for myself, for the feelings that arose and for my journey. My realisation that the pain is not meant to be pushed aside, nor that sorrow or fear will be something we can get over and never feel again, was very freeing.

Suicide, leaving this planet, whilst it was tempting, always brought me back to here now and I knew somewhere inside of me that real peace comes from acknowledging all that we feel with the kindness we would show a hurting child and, more importantly, to know that when joy or love appears at our door, it is as fleeting as sorrow or anger.

To let go of holding on or pushing away means that true transformation can happen. We emerge from our stories into a new life where the meaning of living becomes deeply rooted in allowing our humanity the sacred grace that it deserves and needs.

My life has been very unconventional and because of this it was very easy to get lost in feeling like a failure, not fitting in, not belonging in this world. I often thought someone had dropped me onto the wrong planet many times over, but even now as I enter another time of not knowing who I am, where I am going in life, in my early forties, after ending a big mental health radio station project, for the first time at the end of what would have been perceived a tremendous failure in the past, I see only appreciation. I feel pride in what I had accomplished and in my knowing that with each ending comes a new beginning; and that all perceived failures are not failures, but successful stepping stones on the road to who we are growing into and becoming.

We can never know where this life will take us unless we choose to continue on. What may look like a painful ending, be it a relationship, a job or business, a health challenge, could be the exact journey our souls need to take to become exactly who we are here to be in this lifetime. So, for this reason, while thoughts of suicide may arise from the pain of depression and other mental health issues, we need to keep going and to know that life is very wise, even if our human minds may think otherwise at times.

We were not born into this world broken or as a mistake. We just need to look at the rest of the world and see that everything and everyone has its place in life, from the clouds in the sky to the creatures at the bottom of the ocean. Nature is one beautiful grand design and we are part of this design.

Keep walking, one step at a time. It never ends and neither do you. Trust that what is happening in your life at this moment is sharing with you some wisdom that you may not be able to understand right now, but you will, at exactly the right time.

**About Kelly:**

I'm Kelly Martin, an author, blogger and mental health podcaster who lives in Gloucester in the UK. One of my greatest passions is to help people feel good enough exactly as they are right now.

You can follow me at my mental health blog Kelly Martin Speaks https://kellymartinspeaks.co.uk or subscribe to my mental health podcast Kelly Martin Speaks on iTunes here https://itunes.apple.com/gb/podcast/kelly-martin-speaks/id1376556090

On my journey through the darkness of depression, I have also published two books to support people who feel lost or like a failure in life (more coming soon!). Visit my author website at http://www.kellymartin.co.uk to find out more.

*If you'd like to keep up to date with what Kelly is doing, you can follow her on social media at:*

*Facebook - https://www.facebook.com/KellyMartinSpeaks*

*Twitter - https://twitter.com/KellyMartin_UK*

*You Tube - https://www.youtube.com/user/KellyMartinSpeaks*

*Instagram - https://www.instagram.com/kellymartinspeaks*

# Resources for Suicide

## Suicide and Crisis Helplines, Text and Web services- UK

Samaritans National Lifeline UK & Ireland:

116 123 (UK & Ireland) | Email jo@samaritans.org

Whatever you're going through, call the Samaritans free anytime, from any phone on 116 123.

There is someone there to answer the phone 24 hours a day, 365 days a year. This number is FREE to call. You don't have to be suicidal to call the Samaritans.

Papyrus HOPELine UK:

Call: 0800 068 41 41 - Mon-Fri: 10am-10pm, weekends: 2pm-10pm & bank holidays: 2pm-5pm | Email: pat@papyrus-uk.org | SMS: 07786 209697

HOPELineUK is a specialist telephone service staffed by trained professionals who give non-judgemental support, practical advice and information to: Children, teenagers and young people up to the age of 35 who are worried about how they are feeling

SupportLine UK:

Call the Helpline: 01708 765200 (hours vary so

ring for details)| email: info@supportline.org.uk |
Also Help Resources

They offer confidential emotional support to
children, young adults and adults by telephone,
email and post. They work with callers to develop
healthy, positive coping strategies, an inner feeling
of strength and increased self-esteem to encourage
healing, recovery and moving forward with life.

Saneline: can offer emotional support on 0300 304
7000 (4.30pm-10.30pm every day of the year)

Suicide Crisis: If you live in Gloucestershire http://
www.suicidecrisis.co.uk

CALM: Specifically offering support for men.
Open 5pm - midnight, Call: 0800 585858 or join a
webchat at: https://www.thecalmzone.net

The Mix: http://www.themix.org.uk

The Mix's Crisis Messenger text service is available
24/7 and open to anyone aged 25 or under living
in the UK. If you're in crisis and need to talk, text
THEMIX to 85258.

The Mix has a Webchat and Helpline service
for free and confidential information and help
on a wide range of issues for 13 to 25 year olds
including: sex and relationships, your body, mental
health, drink and drugs, housing, money, work and
study and crime and safety .

Helpline: 0800 808 4994

MIND's Online support chat forum:
https://www.elefriends.org.uk

Inner Compass: moving away from diagnosis /
coming off medication support:
https://www.theinnercompass.org

Hub of Hope: To find resources in your area
https://hubofhope.co.uk

**Aligned organisations and International support:**

SOBS: https://uksobs.org

Suicide Bereavement UK: https://papyrus-uk.org/
suicide-bereavement-support/

Cruse:
https://www.cruse.org.uk/get-help/traumatic-
bereavement/suicide

Metanoia: https://www.metanoia.org/suicide/

Mental Health Foundation:
www.mentalhealth.org.uk/a-to-z/s/suicide

Find a therapist in the UK:
https://www.rscpp.co.uk

Find a therapist in the USA:
https://www.therapyden.com

Mad in America:
https://www.madinamerica.com

A Disorder for Everyone:
http://www.adisorder4everyone.com

Compassionate Mental Health:
http://compassionatementalhealth.co.uk

Lifeline Australia:
https://www.lifeline.org.au/get-help/topics/suicide-bereavement

Heads Together: https://www.headstogether.org.uk

**Online forums:**

Shades of Awakening:
http://shadesofawakening.com (Facebook group)

Drop the Disorder: https://www.facebook.com/groups/1182483948461309/ (Facebook group)

**Online Peer Support Groups:**

The Death Cafe: https://deathcafe.com

IANDS online: https://isgo.iands.org or

http://spiritualemergenceanonymous.org/meetings/

**Retreats and Safe Spaces:**

Safely Held Spaces:
https://www.safelyheldspaces.org

Wales, UK:
http://www.dolifor-centre.com Email: retreats@
innerlife.org.uk or telephone: 01597 810168

**Helpful Reading / Viewing recommended by Contributors**

**Books:**

*The Transformative Power of Near-Death Experiences*,
Dr Penny Sartori and Kelly Walsh

*Mend the Gap*, Katie Mottram

*In Case of Spiritual Emergency*, Catherine G Lucas

*Farther Shores*, Yvonne Kason MD

*Breaking Down is Waking Up*, Dr Russell Razzaque

*Out of the Darkness: From Turmoil to Transformation*, Steve Taylor

*You can Heal Your Life*, Louise Hay

*A Return to Love*, Marianne Williamson

*The Hero's Journey*, Joseph Campbell

*The Power of Now*, Eckhart Tolle

*Conversations with God*, Neale Donald Walsch

*Lost Connections*, Johann Hari

*Reasons to stay alive*, Matt Haig

*Suicide and the Soul*, Hillman

*The Wizard of Earthsea*, Ursula Le Guin

*Let me tell you a story*, Jorge Bucay

*I never promised you a rose garden,* Joanne Greenberg

*Own Your Self: The Surprising Path beyond Depression, Anxiety, and Fatigue to Reclaiming Your Authenticity, Vitality, and Freedom*, Kelly Brogan MD

*The little prince,* Micheal Morpurgo

*Life Crisis*, Catherine G Lucas

Find more listed here:
https://www.wholeheartedpath.com/recommended-books  and http://www.adisorder4everyone.com/books/

**Films:**

*CRAZYWISE* documentary

*#Emerging Proud* film

*Healing Voices*

*The S Word*

*The Stranger on the Bridge*:
www.thestrangeronthebridge.com

**Podcasts / videos:**

*The Happy Place* - Fearne Cotton

*Eleanor Longden; The Voices in my Head*, TED talk on YouTube

Jason Silva: *Shots of Awe* on YouTube

*The resources in the above lists are taken from those indicated as helpful by the #Emerging Proud community when consulted specifically for this project. They are examples, and by no means meant as an exclusive list.

# Self-Care Tips

A crisis is different for everyone, but one thing is the same for all of us; when we are in crisis we can feel as though everything is falling apart.

These tips aim to give you some simple but vital tools that can help you to stay safe and manage your thoughts and feelings.

Having our experiences validated as 'normal', real, natural and meaningful can be one of the most important aspects of being able to heal and grow.

It's vital that we are kind to ourselves during this time, and allow any emotions to surface and be expressed in a safe environment.

Having peer support from someone who has gone through similar experiences, and can listen without judgement, is really helpful. Go to the resources section to find services that may be most helpful for you personally.

You are not alone! What you are going through is a normal part of a healing process. Don't give up – there is a light at the end of the tunnel, even when you feel in complete darkness.

You are not crazy, the healing journey is a painful process, but one well worth embarking on.

**Quick Tips to keep yourself safe:**

Remember that your thoughts do not have to take charge - you can have them without acting on them

If you are feeling like hurting yourself, wait, even if it's for 5 minutes, but just wait, and breathe slow and deep...This may be hard but it's likely the intensity will subside

Call a person or group you can trust to open up to about how you feel

Find a safe environment e.g. with a therapist or in a group, to help you work through trauma when it arises to be healed. Releasing your emotions; verbally, physically and in any other way necessary is vital

Find a safe way to express any emotions that are surfacing

Focus on your self-care - Getting physical exercise / being in nature / eating wholesome food and getting plenty of sleep is important. Initially, some prescribed medications may be necessary to help you manage your life

Avoid stimulants (alcohol / drugs / caffeine / processed foods, especially sugar)

Join a support group – this can be an online forum, it helps not to isolate yourself. Try to find at least one person you trust who you can openly talk to about your experiences without fear of being judged

Listen to calming or uplifting music, and also listening to the sounds of nature can be helpful

Relationships - spend time with supportive people, and distance yourself from ones that feel stressful

Creative self-expression is helpful when you find talking difficult, e.g. drawing, painting, poetry, music, drumming, sculpture, singing

Call a helpline and talk about how you feel, e.g. the Samaritans (number in Resources section)

**Exercise**

Some people find vigorous exercise, like running, very helpful because of the increased amount of energy they are experiencing in their bodies. Others find gentle walking or yoga to be more what they need. Creative exercise e.g. Dancing, Drumming, or even Hula-hooping, can help to release some energy from your body. Let your body move in whatever ways feel natural to you...

## Spiritual Practices

At the beginning of a crisis it's advisable to stop or at least reduce any spiritual practices, e.g. meditation, to slow down your process; these can then be gradually re-introduced over time.

## Stress

It's very common to experience high levels of anxiety during these times. This can present as shallow breathing, palpitations, sweating, confusion or even panic attacks. There are some simple and effective self-help tools that can help you manage these, like a guided body scan, e.g. the Autogenic Technique. Remember also the basic tips on relaxation included in the sleep section, and the benefits gained from releasing emotions and talking openly to someone you trust.

## Creativity and Self-Expression

Many people find times of crisis to also be a time when their creative energies are active. Painting, drawing, craftwork; these can be used as a way of expressing experiences, releasing emotions and bringing a sense of focus. Enjoy the creation of whatever comes, rather than focusing on the final outcome; messy is good!

Dancing, movement, singing and playing music, can create an enormous release of energy. Even when having a bad day, listening to your favourite music and dancing around has an enormous power of positive refocusing. Turn the music up loud and let out those pent-up screams too; it can be very cathartic to release repressed emotions.

Simple things like writing stories, poetry, upcycling old furniture or clothing, changing your bedroom around, all help with creative expression.

Go slow - Small steps can have a big impact, especially when they lead to a growing sense of satisfaction and confidence.

**Suicidal thoughts and Self-Harm**

Even though a crisis can be growth towards healing, there may be times when it is extremely dark, terrifying, and dangerous; it is common to experience having suicidal thoughts and thoughts of self-harm.

There are, however, a lot of things that can help manage this distress, more of which can be found on this link: https://www.metanoia.org/suicide/.

The fact is you are not alone: other people have felt deep and terrible pain and come through it and you can too.

Feeling suicidal does not have to mean giving up on life.

If you are feeling suicidal it may be that you are desperate for things to be different. Wanting this life to end doesn't rule out the possibility of a new, better life beginning, but you may feel like that is beyond reach right now. Imagine what a better life might look like and see how it is possible to realise it if you stick around to find out what could happen. Turn some of that suicidal energy towards risking change in your life. Consider that it may be a behaviour pattern or life condition that you want to end. Ask yourself, 'What inside me needs to die?'

**Some ideas for good self-care:**

1. Embodying practices: Sometimes, our mental chatter can be overbearing and make us feel heavy and overwhelmed. Embodying practices, such as humming, singing, chanting, dancing, yoga, mindfulness and BREATHING, not only bring us in to the present moment, giving us a chance to create space between thoughts.

2. Create a sacred space, be it an altar where you keep things that are meaningful to you, or a room that is your safe haven and your chance to reconnect with yourself.

3. Spend time in nature, whether it's by the sea, a woodland, or even just some fresh air outside your house or your office, spending time in the natural world not only brings us freedom but can reconnect

us to our presence, our aliveness.

4. Practice Gratitude. However hard it may be, try to take a moment to look at all the things you have to be thankful for in your life. Be grateful for the smallest of things, maybe things you take for granted. Be grateful for your bed? Maybe that you have a roof over your head? Maybe you have access to food and clean water? Starting small and working up, inviting more gratitude into your life can transform the way you see and show up in life. This is scientifically proven to rewire our brain.

5. Build up your inner wellspring of self-worth. Whether it be writing down an affirmation and sticking it to your bathroom mirror, creating an empowering and uplifting mantra to chant to yourself every morning, surrounding yourself with people who remind you of your innate worthiness, smiling at yourself when you catch your reflection, listening to uplifting music that makes you feel powerful and ready to take on the world, becoming aware of those inner critics that try to keep you small… whatever it may be, try to create a life that reflects your innate worthiness back to you. Your self-worth does NOT depend on what your profession might or might not be, it doesn't depend on how much you please other people…it is innately yours and it is already within you.

6. Become aware of what's energising you and what is draining you. Say YES to the things that energise and nurture you and NO to the things that drain

your energy or no longer serve you. Set boundaries! This is easier said than done sometimes, we highly recommend *Braving the Wilderness* by Brené Brown for guidance on setting healthy boundaries.

7. Thank Your Body for all the things it does for you every second of every day. While you are reading this, your heart is pumping, your lungs are breathing, your digestive system is working to turn the food you ate earlier into energy, your cells are being healed and renewed. There are thousands of biochemical reactions happening that we have no say in, our body does that on its own. Let's thank it for what it does for us and allows us to do.

8. Read. Take a look at our recommended reading list in the Resources section of this book for some empowering and life-changing reading.

9. Create with your heart. Creativity can come in as many different forms as there are people in this world, whether it's writing, dancing, painting, sculpting, singing... tap into those creative juices running through you. Try focusing on the process of creating as opposed to the end product...get messy, have a play and tap into your inner child.

10. Trust the healing process. The road to recovery is not always a linear one, sometimes it's a case of taking one step forward and two steps back and that's ok.

11. Connect with supportive and inspiring people, who are willing to listen without judgement and an open heart. If you can't find them in person, join an online group.

12. Find a safe space to be vulnerable, to speak your truth, express your feelings. Maybe with a therapist or a mentor.

13. Join a support group. Connect with people who are going through similar things and build each other up.

14. Diversify your social media feed. All day, every day we are bombarded with images from different kinds of screens. Much of the time, images that have been edited and tampered with. Taking control of what we are seeing can drastically improve our mental health and wellbeing. Choosing to see more positive posts will not only allow your brain to create new neural pathways and create a new 'normal', but you will feel more uplifted and at peace with yourself.

15. Celebrate every success. Sometimes all these things can seem too much or even unimaginable to do. Sometimes self-care comes in the form of getting out of bed in the morning, cleaning your teeth, having a wash...Give yourself a pat on the back and celebrate every success you can. You are doing an amazing job and we are so proud of you for not giving up!

You can do this!

*"Hold on tight! The sun will shine again and you will be glad you never let go."*

*Kelly Walsh*

# Acknowledgements

My infinite thanks go to the incredible Kinda Proud team; the book Reps, and especially Kelly Walsh for spearheading, and Mandy Horne for editing, this particular edition in the series. Our Publisher Sean Patrick of *That Guy's House* and PR Consultant Jenna Owen of *Media Jems*, all of whom have passionately, and without question, donated their time and expertise in order to support this project to fruition. It's a vision we all share, and one that would not have been possible to achieve without each and every one of us coming together with no agenda other than wanting to disseminate hope like confetti around the world...

The team also extends our immense gratitude to everyone in this pocket book, who have bravely gifted their personal transformation story with the hope that it helps at least one other person in the world to find their own inner spark to initiate or aid their recovery journey. We aim for these books to create a 'positive domino effect', rippling out HOPE to those who need it most.

Our gratitude also goes to The Missing Kind charity who seed-funded this project as an official Sponsor, and *ISEN (the International Spiritual Emergence Network) for allowing us to use information from their crisis guide in our self-care tips section.

Without all of these team players there would be no HOPE confetti, so together we celebrate the incredible power of heart-founded collaboration, and a shared vision and mission.

# The Kinda Proud Team

Other titles in our Kinda Proud Pocket Books of Hope and Transformation series so far

#Emerging Proud through NOTEs (non-ordinary transcendent experiences)

#Emerging Proud through Disordered Eating, Body Image and Low Self-Esteem

#Emerging Proud through Trauma and Abuse

# Hope

**It's all I need
to lift my heart
out of the depths
and into the light**

**— Ambriel**